ENRICHING DEVOTIONALS
FROM THE PSALMS

ENTERING
HIS
COURTS

STEVE
GALLAGHER

PURE LIFE MINISTRIES
14 School Street
Dry Ridge, KY 41035
(888) PURELIFE - to order
www.purelifeministries.org

ENTERING HIS COURTS:
Enriching Devotionals from the Psalms

ISBN/EAN # 978-0-9800286-7-6
eBook ISBN/EAN # 978-0-9854421-3-2

BIBLE TRANSLATIONS

Scripture quotations are marked with abbreviations as noted below after each verse or portion of verse in which they are used. They are all taken from the Holy Bible in the following translations and are listed here in order of usage. We acknowledge that all scripture quotations taken from these translations are the sole property of the respective publisher and all permission rights are reserved by them. They are used here by permission.

Contents

INTRODUCTION

It was early in 2010 that I undertook one of the most enriching Bible studies I have ever done. That's when I tackled the nearly 2,500 verses of the book of Psalms. I began by going over each verse in at least a dozen translations and paraphrases and writing out those which stated the verse in the most compelling manner. This took nearly six months to accomplish.* Next I went all the way back to the beginning—Psalm One—and studied each psalm verse by verse through different commentaries, most notably Charles Spurgeon's excellent work, *The Treasury of David.*

The accumulative effect on my spiritual life was tremendous. There were many days that it seemed as if the very life of God was flowing into my inner being through the rich text I was studying. Some days I would literally spend hours in it—unable to pull myself away from it! It truly left a deep imprint upon my soul.

In my Bible study entitled, *He Leads Me Beside Still Waters*, I wrote the following regarding the book of Psalms:

> Through it all one cannot escape the fact that the book of Psalms is an utterly candid compilation of the mental struggles of these different men; of their varying seasons of joy, anguish and despair; of their highest hopes and deepest

---

* This compilation of various translations for each verse is available as *Selah! The Book of Psalms in the Richest Translations.*

fears; of their conflicts or even failures with sin; of their disgust for self-serving flatterers and their compassion for the needy; and most of all, for their overarching appreciation for the Lord's sovereign involvement in their lives.

The book of Psalms is a treasure chest of the most profound interactions between pious men and a loving, caring God. David, its most prominent writer, was called a man after God's own heart. What could be more beneficial and rewarding than to contemplate his times of intimate communion with a holy God?

As I soaked in this marvelous compilation of ancient prayers through various translations, I found myself uncovering new treasures at an astonishing rate. It's no wonder I had such a difficult time withdrawing from my study time—the thought that I might discover a new nugget of truth in the next verse kept me diligently searching.

I became so blessed by these many nuggets of truth that I began writing them down. I did this for the sheer enjoyment of it and never thought about it going any further than that. But someone suggested the truths I had discovered could make a wonderful devotional for other people. Well, I'll let you be the judge of that. All I can say is that I was greatly blessed in this undertaking and I hope you will be as well!

As you read the selections, you'll find at the end of each day several thought provoking and heart searching questions. I encourage you to take time to pray and meditate over these, allowing God to search your heart and to listening for His response to you. There are also pages inserted for you to write down your own thoughts and perhaps even prayers of commitment to Him. My prayer is that you will find yourself truly enriched by *Entering His Courts*.

WEEK
ONE

Week One: MONDAY

They are Called "Devotions" For A Reason

*"My heart is steadfast, O God, my heart is steadfast; I will
sing, yes, I will sing praises! Awake, my glory! Awake,
harp and lyre! I will awaken the dawn." (Psalm 57:7-8)*

David was running for his life when he penned these words. It's possible he felt that he needed to rouse himself up to maintain his devotional life, but his story clearly shows that for years before this he had already maintained a solid time with God every morning.

Generally speaking, American Christians have been able to get by without much of a connection with God. Life has been good in the United States. But I believe those days are coming to an end. When calamity is striking from every side is *not* the time to attempt to establish a solid devotional life. When times of distress come, a person who is not accustomed to a solid connection with God is going to come unraveled. It is so much wiser to get one's devotional life in order during times of peace than to attempt to do it when "all hell is breaking loose" against believers!

The word "steadfast" in Psalm 57:7 (Heb. *kun*) is rendered "fixed" in some translations. This is a man who had determined—above all else— to have a time of worship, praise and prayer with God every morning. This kind of commitment is the key to establishing an important habit like prayer. In a certain sense, it is very comparable to quitting smoking. Making the resolute decision to stop the habit is half the battle. What makes the experience so unnecessarily miserable is when the person constantly waffles back and forth with his commitment.

So it is with establishing a prayer life. Once a person has made a firm consecration to doing this—no matter what distractions the enemy might throw at him—he is halfway there! Notice David's commitment: "I will sing… I will sing praises!… I will awaken the dawn." I will! I will! I will! He expressed this same sentiment on another occasion when he said, "In the morning, O Lord, *You will* hear my voice; in the morning *I will* order *my prayer* to You and *eagerly* watch." (Psalm 5:3)

It will take this kind of resolute determination to get one's prayer life established. Someone once said, "Satan laughs at our toiling, mocks at our wisdom, but trembles when we pray."[1] It is for this very reason that he and his minions do their utmost to discourage believers from praying. Watchman Nee wrote: "When we pray with such prayer, our prayer will shake up hell and affect Satan. For this reason, Satan will rise up to hinder such prayer. All prayers which come from God touch the powers of darkness. Here involves spiritual warfare. Perhaps our physical bodies, our families, or whatever pertains to us will be attacked by Satan. For whenever there is such prayer, it calls for Satanic assault. The enemy so attacks in order that our prayer might be discontinued."[2]

We must be determined to overcome all the distractions and attacks the enemy will hurl our way. Once they see that you consider your devotional time to be inviolable, they will grow discouraged and give up.

Yes, there is a reason they are called "devotions." You must be truly devoted to Christ to stay faithful to your daily devotions.

And how about you?

- *Have you made this kind of commitment to spending quality time with the Lord? Do you faithfully seek His face every morning?*
- *Can He count on you to intercede for the lost?*
- *Does your daily life reveal a true devotion to Christ?*

Preparing Your Heart

*"My heart is steadfast, O God, my heart is steadfast; I will
sing, yes, I will sing praises! Awake, my glory! Awake, harp
and lyre! I will awaken the dawn." (Psalm 57:7-8)*

I n yesterday's devotional, we took a brief glimpse at the word
"steadfast" in Psalm 57:7 (Heb. *kun*). This Hebraic term is also
used in the sense of preparation. For instance, of the Israelites who
wandered in the wilderness with Moses for forty years, the psalmist
said that they were "A stubborn and rebellious generation, a generation
that did not prepare its heart and whose spirit was not faithful to
God." (Psalm 78:8) In contradistinction to this wayward generation, King
Hezekiah would later pronounce a special blessing on a certain group
of Israelites: "May the good Lord pardon everyone who prepares his
heart to seek God…" (2 Chronicles 30:18-19)

Elsewhere I wrote the following:

"The important position the heart occupies within a
person can be seen in Scripture… People are told to 'rend' their
hearts (Joel 2:12), seek God with all their hearts (Psalm 119:2, 10),
and pour out their hearts before Him. (Psalm 62:8) We are told
of those who deceive their own hearts (James 1:26), backslide
in heart (Proverbs 14:14), spurn reproof in their hearts (Proverbs
5:12), and regard wickedness in their hearts. (Psalm 66:18) It's no
wonder then that we are admonished to, 'Keep thy heart with

all diligence; for out of it are the issues of life.' (Proverbs 4:23 KJV) Surely it is true: 'the inward thought and the heart of a man are deep.'" (Psalm 64:6)

Preparing one's heart to meet with the Lord is an important aspect of maintaining a quality devotional life. The truth is that the heart of man has a natural propensity toward sin, selfishness and pride. Spiritual pursuits do not come naturally to us. We must prepare our hearts to seek the Lord.

The other interesting word found in today's passage of Scripture is "glory." Why would David be speaking of his own glory? The Hebrew word literally means "weighty." From there it is used to describe someone of substantial character. Of course, this term is rightly used repeatedly of the Lord. I believe Spurgeon captured the right idea when he said the following about this phrase: "Let the noblest powers of my nature bestir themselves: the intellect which conceives thought, the tongue which expresses it, and the inspired imagination which beautifies it - let all be on the alert now that the hour for praise has come."[3]

AND HOW ABOUT YOU?

- *Do you consider your relationship with God valuable enough to prepare your heart to meet with Him?*
- *Does He mean enough to you that you will gather together all of your most noble aspirations to praise His name?*

Notes

Stern Correction

"The Lord has corrected me sternly, but He has not abandoned me to destruction." (Psalm 118:18 Har)

It should go without saying that the Lord handles newborn Christians with "kid gloves." They cannot handle much so the Lord tends to shield them from overwhelming difficulties. A boxing manager would not throw his new fighter into the ring with a seasoned veteran; a mother would not send her toddler across a busy thoroughfare by himself; and the Lord doesn't put His baby believers into situations they are not yet prepared to handle.

However, correction is as much a part of the Christian maturing process as it is for the young child. Solomon could have been talking about the Lord's dealings with His people when he wrote, "If you refuse to discipline your son, it proves you don't love him; for if you love him, you will be prompt to punish him... A youngster's heart is filled with rebellion, but punishment will drive it out of him." (Proverbs 13:24; 22:15 LB) And, as the writer of Hebrews later pointed out: "If God doesn't punish you when you need it, as other fathers punish their sons, then it means that you aren't really God's son at all—that you don't really belong in his family." (Hebrews 12:8 LB)

As members of a race of rebels, there is much within us that must be corrected. If we are left to ourselves, we will nearly always tend to think, speak and act in a way that characterizes the fallen nature. The very fact that it comes so "naturally" points out the need to have our mindset continually adjusted. The Lord uses different tools to accomplish this, but, by and large, the most effective means He has to help us to acquire the mind of Christ is through various forms of discipline.

There are those times that we are disciplined because we have committed some outright sin. But just as often, we must "go out to the woodshed" simply as part of the maturing process. Sometimes those bouts of discipline can be very severe. While we fragile humans can't handle too much adversity, the Lord knows far better than we how powerfully effective such times are in changing our natures. There are some times when the Vinekeeper must prune the branch all the way back to the Vine. And yet, it is this very kind of severe pruning that always produces the most bountiful crop.

While there are those occasions when the discipline seems to be so overwhelming that the person despairs of life itself, there is an inherent promise found in the psalmist's testimony: "Yes, the Lord has disciplined me severely, *but* He will never allow me to be destroyed by it." In fact, it could easily be argued that His desire to save us from destruction is one of His primary reasons for allowing the discipline in the first place.

As difficult as the Christian life can be at times, what is the alternative? I would rather the Lord thrash me to an inch of my life; nay, I would rather He allowed me to die a violent death, than for Him to allow me to destroy myself through sin and rebellion.

And how about you?

- *How do you respond when the Lord brings correction into your life?*
- *Have you learned to see the value of it, or are you still at an early developmental stage of resisting the process?*

Week One: THURSDAY

A Blueprint For Worship

> *"O God in Zion, we wait before you in silent praise, and thus fulfill our vow. How greatly to be envied are those you have chosen to come and live with you within the holy tabernacle courts! What joys await us among all the good things there."* (Psalm 65:1, 4 LB)

It's Sunday morning and the home of Jim and Janet Smith is a picture of bustling activity. Having gotten ready for church, they turn their attention to the needs of their three children—getting them showered, dressed and fed. Eventually, the family is making their harried drive to church. The scene at their house of worship is amazingly similar to home. Kids are running around the foyer, playing and frolicking. Women huddle together gabbing about their kids, while their husbands discuss the plight of their favorite sports team. The music emerging from the sanctuary brings the conversations to a forced conclusion and, having retrieved their children, they make their way to their seats.

Allow me to present for your consideration a typical Sunday morning service at Pure Life Ministries (PLM). The seventy or so men in the residential program are required to be in the sanctuary 30-60 minutes before the service begins. There they sit in absolute silence until the worship service begins. This routine is a wonderful discipline to men who have allowed their lives to spiral out of control to the point of engaging in illicit sexual behavior. To be required to resist the natural tendency to talk, joke and laugh before service is an entirely new discipline for these men.

23

While this restraint provides its own benefits, there are other reasons for this practice. First, there is a great gulf between singing hymns and choruses by rote and truly worshiping God from the heart. "God is spirit," said Jesus, "and those who worship Him must worship in spirit and truth." (John 4:24) If we are going to go through the motions of worshiping God, we *must* do it in the Spirit (as opposed to the flesh) and in truth (as opposed to contrived and insincere devotion). Realistically, the only way such worship can take place is for a person to quiet himself; to subdue his flesh so that he can be properly prepared to offer sincere, Spirit-led worship to God.

Secondly, it is proper to approach the Most High God with a reverential attitude. I believe that one of the reasons sin is running rampant in the Church is that people have increasingly become familiar with holy things. It's not uncommon anymore to hear the Lord spoken of disrespectfully, *e.g.,* "Jesus is my bud!" How much better it is to approach God with the holy fear that befits the situation.

Having been in at least a thousand such meetings at PLM, I can testify that when we begin to worship the Lord, it is real, it is meaningful and it is sincere. Visitors are amazed at how God's presence is so tangible in the Pure Life chapel. Is it because we are better than others? No, I believe it simply because we approach the Lord with the respect He is due.

AND HOW ABOUT YOU?

- *Can you see how it would help your walk with God to quiet yourself before going to church?*
- *Are you willing to commit yourself to approaching future worship times with a quiet spirit, a loving heart and a reverential attitude?*

Secret of the Lord

"Friendship with God is reserved for those who reverence
him. With them alone he shares the secrets of his promises."
(Psalm 25:14 LB)

For those who understand ancient Middle Eastern culture, there is a clear picture being presented in David's statement above. Before we present that image, we must briefly consider the life of royalty.

Typically speaking, the common man would only see his nation's king in controlled settings. It is possible that he would catch a glimpse of him as he traveled through town surrounded by his aides and bodyguards, but he would be more likely to see the king on his throne. Everything surrounding him in that regal setting is meant to convey the idea that this is a special person. The last thing the king's assistants want is for the commoners to enter that room and see the king on their own level.

The point in all this pageantry is to exalt the king—not so he can somehow feel better about himself—but so his subjects will respect his authority. The average citizen will never see his king under circumstances other than these.

However, every monarch has those close confidants to whom he can share his heart. He has his "joint chiefs of staff," the military leaders whose job it is to defend the country. He also has economic advisors, political consultants and those who specialize in foreign affairs. Each of these people have access to the nation's leader that the common man will never enjoy.

But then there are those with whom the king shares his deepest secrets: his perspectives and attitudes about other leaders, the long-range purposes he holds for his kingdom, the way he handles the great variety of issues of the day he faces.

This is also true in God's kingdom. He too has His favorites. However, there is an amazing difference between an earthly leader and the Almighty. While a president or king confides in old friends and gifted advisors, God opens the door for any commoner to enter that level of intimacy with Him. He leaves it completely up to us: we can have as little or as much fellowship with Him as we desire.

Another difference in the two situations is the quality of people desiring attendance in these two throne rooms. One of the greatest challenges an earthly monarch faces is the difficulty in discerning a person's motives for wanting to be near him. Too often, crafty, ambitious men adept at using flattery and feigned devotion are the ones to gain a position of trust.

This is not the case with our God! Not only does He have personal knowledge of each and every citizen in His kingdom, but He can see past a person's outward show and right into the very motives and attitudes of the heart. As the Lord told Samuel, "God sees not as man sees, for man looks at the outward appearance, but the Lord looks at the heart." (1 Samuel 16:7)

So God can flawlessly choose the ones with whom He wishes to share that level of intimacy. Not only can we rest assured that only those who belong in such a place of honor will be awarded it, but that door is open to all! Every citizen of God's kingdom has the right to such a position if he will only prove it through his reverential devotion to the Lord.

AND HOW ABOUT YOU?

- *Where do you see yourself in God's circle of friends?*

- *Are you willing to consecrate yourself to His kingdom in such a way that He could call you friend?*

Week One: SATURDAY

The Shepherd

"The LORD is my shepherd, I shall not want. He makes me lie down in green pastures; He leads me beside quiet waters. He restores my soul; He guides me in the paths of righteousness for His name's sake." (Psalm 23:1-3)

The beautiful passage above presents two persons: the Shepherd/Lord and the sheep/believer.

Jesus Christ would later use and amplify this illustration to describe His role with His followers. "I am the good shepherd," He said, "and I know My own and My own know Me, even as the Father knows Me and I know the Father..." (John 10:14-15) For Jesus to say that His followers would know Him in the same way the Father does is an extraordinary statement. There is nothing superficial in their relationship. It speaks of a deep intimacy and a meaningful submission of One to the Other.

This is the very characteristic that stands out in the respective roles of the Shepherd and sheep in the Psalm 23 illustration. The Shepherd clearly takes the leading role in the relationship. He leads His sheep into green pastures, alongside quiet waters, down paths of righteousness and ultimately, "through the valley of the shadow of death."

What makes these people follow Him? Is it a religious system they are following? Is it a popular movement they are joining? Are they following a set of rules in the hopes of avoiding hell and going to heaven? No! It is a Person they are following!

Jesus offers a clear explanation of their motivation: "the sheep follow him because they know his voice. A stranger they simply will not

29

follow, but will flee from him, because they do not know the voice of strangers." (John 10:4-5)

Christians don't obey biblical commandments so that they might be considered good enough to inherit God's kingdom. They obey the Lord because they truly love Him and want to please Him. They follow Him, they obey Him and they emulate Him. They have a spiritual connection to God that enables them to discern His will for their daily lives. This is how they know when it is time to get refreshed by the quiet waters or when it is time to hit the trail again!

Psalm 23 offers the different aspects of the believer's life. First and foremost, he must have regular, meaningful times sitting in God's presence. Eating the lush vegetation represents the place Scriptures hold in our lives. The word for "green pastures" (Heb. *deshe*) literally refers to the tender shoots of new grass. It is the most delectable food a sheep can find. This is an apt description of what the Word of God is to the hungry believer.

The "quiet waters" describes the refreshment that comes from spending quality time in the presence of the Holy Spirit. Believers facing the conflicts of life sense their great need for the revitalizing effects of prayer.

The time spent with God is what enables the believer to get back on the path of righteousness. Sometimes it is a lonely path. It is a path fraught with dangers. Around any bend one might encounter some alluring temptress or some savage assault. But as he follows his great Shepherd, he will always have the assurance of being kept on the "straight and narrow."

AND HOW ABOUT YOU?

- *Are you allowing the Lord to lead and direct the affairs of your life, the decisions you make, the direction you are going? Or are you the master of your own ship?*
- *Do you spend quality time with Him so that you can get His leading on your life?*

God's Waiter

*"Behold, as the eyes of servants look to the hand of their
master, as the eyes of a maid to the hand of her mistress,
so our eyes look to the Lord our God, until He is gracious
to us." (Psalm 123:2)*

In 1995 a friend and I were traveling throughout Turkey visiting the ruins of various New Testament cities. One day we stopped for lunch in a Turkish town lying adjacent to ancient Thyatira. Being the only guests in the restaurant that day, our young waiter was able to focus all of his attention upon our needs. I have never seen such a display of attentiveness in all my many years of dining out. He stood at a respectful distance away, but there was no question that he was utterly alert to the slightest gesture we might make to signal some need.

If this can be true with a modern waiter, how much more so for a servant in biblical times whose very life depended upon his master's favor. It is this vivid picture the psalmist paints to convey to his readers what it means to wait upon the Lord.

God has created a dynamic in life whereby any human who so wishes may enter into a covenantal relationship with Him. This pact holds benefits and responsibilities for both parties.

As our master, the Lord has a right to expect our total dedication to His cause, His great purposes and His specific wishes. As His servants, we are expected to fulfill His commands, obey Him implicitly and give Him heartfelt devotion. This relationship is far deeper and more comprehensive than the superficial obedience that pseudo-Christianity suggests. We don't serve a master who lives in a faraway place; one who only expects us to perform our duties nominally. No, we live in the Master's home and are in His presence continually.

This Turkish waiter was one of the few I have ever seen who actually live up to the name of their occupation. He waited. He waited for us to convey our wishes. He waited with the utmost attentiveness. What's more, he waited with an attitude of great respect. This is the proper attitude we should hold of the Most High God.

To "wait upon the Lord" has the sense of quietly sitting in expectation of His word. As the Master, the Lord has the right to choose when He wishes something to be done. As our Commander, He has the right to pick the right time to tell us to move forward. As our heavenly Father, He has the right to respond to our requests in His timing. If we will "watch and pray," God will direct us, lead us and fulfill all of our petitions; and His timing will be perfect. "Blessed is that servant whom his master when he comes shall find so doing!" (Matthew 24:46 WNT)

And how about you?

- *Do you see yourself as God's "waiter?" Or do you see Him as being the one who should serve you?*
- *Have you learned to truly wait on the Lord?*

WEEK
TWO

Restoration

> *"When Yahweh brought Zion's captives home, at first*
> *it seemed like a dream. Then our mouths filled with*
> *laughter and our lips with song. Even the pagans started*
> *talking about the marvels Yahweh had done for us!*
> *What marvels indeed he did for us, and*
> *how overjoyed we were!" (Psalm 126:1-3 JB)*

The occasion of this outburst of joyous memory is found in the first chapter of Ezra where we are told that the Lord "stirred up the spirit of Cyrus king of Persia" to allow the Jewish people to return to their homeland after seventy years of exile in Babylon. One can only imagine the trip home for these refugees when they "walked among the crowds of worshipers, leading a great procession to the house of God, singing for joy and giving thanks amid the sound of a great celebration!" (Psalm 42:4 NLT)

But Psalm 126 also points to a deeper spiritual truth. Throughout Scripture, Babylon is represented as the God-defying world. Although man was created in the image of God, years of languishing in the corrupt environs of Babylon leaves him defiled, scarred and damaged. And those who spend a lifetime under the sway of the god of this world know the abject misery and hopelessness of Babylonian life better than most.

And just like the Jewish exiles restored to their homeland were overjoyed, so too are those who first enter the kingdom of God! Many are so overcome with joy that they cannot contain it. The laughter spoken of here isn't what one would witness in a carnal comedy club or amongst drunks carrying on in foolish revelry. This laughter wells up within the new believer when the joy of the Lord is introduced into his inner being.

And the singing mentioned here is not the carnal merriment found on secular radio, or even the obligatory hymn singing of those who really can't relate to the profound truths they are mouthing. The song spoken of here is the irrepressible gratitude bursting forth from the heart of a person who just been welcomed into the family of God.

For those who have paid dearly to be a slave of Babylon, emancipation brings joy unspeakable—joy beyond words. They remember all too well the abject misery of being held by the cords of sin; of serving a brutal master; of living from one empty pleasure to the next. No wonder their newfound freedom seems like a dream come true!

And how about you?

- *Have you experienced the joy of salvation?*
- *If not, is it because you have never really grasped the inexpressible value of salvation?*
- *Or could it be that you have never really been emancipated?*
- *The answer to these questions is more important than words can express.*

God's Balancing Act

"Give us now as much happiness as the sadness you gave us during all our years of misery." (Psalm 90:15 GNB)

If there is one thing God's people can rest in, it is that He is going to deal with them as a righteous judge. In fact, the preceding psalm says that "Righteousness and justice are the foundation of [God's] throne..." (Psalm 89:14) He is always perfectly balanced in everything He does in our lives. He is a master at knowing how to maintain the perfect equilibrium in all His dealings with us.

Consider the great challenge the Holy Spirit has in managing the lives of individual believers. If He grants us too much prosperity, we tend to become spiritually complacent. Yet He also doesn't want to see His children groveling in abject poverty either. If the Lord encourages us too much, we tend to become independent-minded; but if He chastens us too severely we can easily lapse into self-centered depression. If He gives us opportunities of great ministry, whereby He is able to use us mightily for His kingdom, we tend to become puffed up with pride; but if He doesn't use us at all, we feel like our spiritual life is meaningless. In spite of the enormity of the challenge, the Lord has an uncanny ability to introduce the exact proper mixture of ingredients into our lives to bring about His great purpose for us as believers.

Another aspect of God's balanced approach to our lives is that the greater a person is used in His kingdom, the greater that person's sufferings will tend to be. Of course, there have been well-known ministers who seemed as though everything they touched turned to gold. While their ministries prosper and flourish, other men—better men—struggle along with seemingly little fruit to show for their efforts. Ah, but that's looking on the outward, and man does not see as God sees. Many prosperous ministries make a big splash and accomplish little of eternal value, while some seemingly inconsequential ministries have the full attention of both angels and devils!

Be that as it may, when God is able to use a person to deeply impact the lives of others, I can assure you that much suffering has undergirded it all. How do I know this? Because it is the person who has traveled down the narrow path of adversity and death to the self-life who is most full of God. That being the case, the person who has suffered most can expect the most meaningful fruit to come forth from their lives.

AND HOW ABOUT YOU?

- *Has the Lord allowed you to face a great deal of affliction in life?*

- *Have you tried to avoid suffering or escape affliction?*

- *Have you later realized God desired the suffering or affliction for His good to be accomplished in you, or through you?*

- *Allow me to encourage you to go boldly to His throne of grace and ask Him to bring forth fruit in proportion to your suffering.*

Notes

Week Two: WEDNESDAY

Chaos and Serenity

> *"...though the mountains slip into the heart of the sea; though its waters roar and foam, though the mountains quake at its swelling pride. There is a river whose streams make glad the city of God, the holy dwelling places of the Most High. God is in the midst of her, she will not be moved; God will help her when morning dawns." (Psalm 46:2-5)*

Psalm 46 presents two contrasting scenes. On the one hand, the psalmist could see a world that seemed to be coming apart at the seams. It is a picture of worldwide upheaval; calamities of nature, nations rising and falling and people in great distress. And yet, at the same time, he saw a God who sat enthroned in Heaven, unshakeable, immovable, unchanging and heavily involved in the lives of His people. The one scene is of utter chaos; the other is of absolute serenity.

This psalm, known as Martin Luther's favorite because of all of the instability in Europe during his lifetime, has been a source of comfort and assurance during troublesome times for God's people down through the ages. It offers a bright message of hope in a world that has often gone terribly awry.

If this has been the case in the past, how much more so should it be applicable to our day and age? We are entering a time of such distress "such as has not occurred since the beginning of the creation..." (Mark 13:19) Surely we need to consider the great truth conveyed in this psalm!

We have already witnessed unbelievable calamities upon earth in the past decade. We have watched Muslim fanatics attack the United States.

41

ENTERING HIS COURTS

We are witnessing the beginning stages of a world that has become united against God: "…the nations in an uproar and the… kings of the earth take their stand and the rulers take counsel together against the Lord and against His Anointed…" (Psalm 2:1-2)

Head knowledge about spiritual things will not get us through the dark days ahead. A superficial relationship with God will not suffice. We need a fresh revelation of the Most High God calmly sitting on His throne, overlooking the affairs of man. It is time that we begin to earnestly ask God to reveal Himself to us. He will open our hearts if we will only ask.

AND HOW ABOUT YOU?

- *Do you have your head buried in the sand regarding the perilous times in which we live? If so, it is time to calmly take an honest look at what is happening in the world in relation to biblical prophecy.*

- *Or perhaps you are looking at the future with a fretful heart? If so, obey the words of Jesus: "But when these things begin to take place, straighten up and lift up your heads, because your redemption is drawing near." (Luke 21:28)*

Lions and Apostates

> *"Oh, put God to the test and see how kind he is! See for yourself the way his mercies shower down on all who trust in him. If you belong to the Lord, reverence him; for everyone who does this has everything he needs. Even strong young lions sometimes go hungry, but those of us who reverence the Lord will never lack any good thing."* (Psalm 34:8-10 LB)

T he young lion instinctively understands that he is the king of the beasts. His unflinching stride, craftiness as a hunter and terrifying roar all bespeak an animal that possesses an unwavering degree of self-confidence.

The Living Bible rightly uses the word "lions," as that is the literal term for the Hebrew word *kephîyr*. But it would be good to remember that the word lion is also employed—in all languages—to describe people. In fact, a quick scan through a thesaurus offers quite a few interesting synonyms: man of courage, conqueror, big shot, great man, dignitary, etc. Thus, it is more understandable why other Bible versions use figurative language in their interpretations of this verse:

- The renegade may be in need, and go hungry... (Har)
- Apostates may be famishing and starving…(Mof)
- Rich men have become poor and hungry… (Sept)

The truth of the matter is that the powerful lion is an apt illustration of capable people in this world—most especially those who feel no need to rely on God; people such as renegades, apostates and rich men.

Like the great cat, such people develop a strong sense of confidence at an early age. Driven by ambition and dreams of success, they throw themselves into their chosen occupations with all the energy their youth has to offer. Their level of confidence grows until they come to believe that they can surmount any obstacle, rise to any challenge and push through their own agenda in any situation.

Past successes make them oblivious to their human frailty. They don't seem to realize that at any time they could contract a debilitating disease, face an unexpected economic setback or even be struck down with an untimely death. Their temporal fate lies completely at the whim of a world which can be very cruel. In the end, self-reliant people feel no need for God's help; therefore they will receive none.

What a sharp contrast they are with the "poor and needy" who must cry out for God's aid. Their condition does not necessarily mean that they are incompetent or insecure. This poverty of spirit simply means that they have learned that they desparately need God's help and that He can be counted on to provide it.

David claims that all who reverence God will be well cared for. Perhaps the best way to describe the difference between such people and the self-reliant lies in their perspective of God. The Lord is very tiny in the minds of those who are brimming with self-confidence. They are full of themselves and have little room left over for God or anyone else. On the other hand, God looms very large in the heart of those who fear Him.

The truth is that God-fearing souls are the joy of the Lord's heart. He truly loves to shower His mercies "down on all who trust in him."

Let us put everything that concerns us today into His trustworthy hands and watch as He takes good care of our lives.

AND HOW ABOUT YOU?

- *Where does your trust lie?*

- *Are you strong in yourself and weak in Christ , or weak in yourself and strong in Christ?*

- *I realize you have "trusted Christ for salvation," but have you yet come to know what it means to trust Him for the details of your daily life?*

The Way of the Lord

*"Make me know Thy ways, O Lord; teach me Thy paths.
Lead me in Thy truth..." (Psalm 25:4-5a)*

Scripture repeatedly describes the believer's life as a journey which will take place on a path prescribed by the Lord. This odyssey is not traveled in the realm of space—as if the person is moving from one physical locale to another—it occurs in the realm of time. The trip begins at rebirth and goes on until the person's existence on earth has been terminated.

Wherever we live on this planet, whatever our employment and family situation might be, there is a "way" to live our lives that has been prescribed by Scripture. It is the "way of the Lord." In other words, the lifestyle we lead should reflect God's character; and should do so increasingly as we go.

In today's verse we see David making three requests of the Lord. First, he asks God to help him to know His ways. This is a worthy prayer for anyone desirous of being a *follower* of the Lord. Several hundred years prior to this Moses had prayed, "Now therefore, I pray You, if I have found favor in Your sight, let me know Your ways that I may know You, so that I may find favor in Your sight." (Exodus 33:13) Moses and David—perhaps the two most distinguished believers of the Old Testament—asked God for the same thing: they wanted to have intimate, personal knowledge of His manner of life; His perspectives, behavior and so on. In short, they wanted to know His character.

The second part of David's petition is the request to be taught His paths. I tend to think this is where the prayer turns more personal. God has a path laid out for each of His people from long before they were even born. It is His will for their life and all that that signifies. Charles Spurgeon said, "Unsanctified natures clamor for their own way, but gracious spirits cry, 'Not my will, but thine be done.'"

The last phrase expresses David's desire to be personally conducted along life's road. He is not satisfied with mere teachings; he wants a personal tour guide who will show him every step of the way in which he should walk. This guide is one of the pillars of God's character: His infallible Truth. If a person can stay within the boundaries of Truth, everything in life will work out well.

It would do us all well if we kept this three-part petition—or some form of it—in our daily prayers. "Lord make me to know Your behavior patterns; reveal Your will for my life; guide me along life's way within the confines of Your great reality."

And how about you?

- *Can you see the need to seek God in this way?*
- *Are you willing to commit to incorporating these requests into your daily prayer life?*
- *Why not do so now?*

Week Two: SATURDAY

Traps and Pitfalls

> *"O Lord, fight those fighting me; declare war on them for their attacks on me... Blow them away like chaff in the wind—wind sent by the Angel of the Lord. Make their path dark and slippery before them, with the Angel of the Lord pursuing them. For though I did them no wrong, yet they laid a trap for me and dug a pitfall in my path." (Psalm 35:1, 5-7 LB)*

Yesterday we looked at the believer's lifelong journey. Today we will extend that analogy out to consider some of the "dangers, toils and snares" that believers are certain to encounter along the path of life.

Our lifetime is a long road which is overseen by the Lord. Nothing escapes His notice. Since He abides in the eternal realm—outside the realm of Time—in one glance He can view everything that has or will occur in our lives. It is comforting to know that the Lord takes such care for His children.

But there are other eyes scrutinizing our lives as well—hate-filled eyes. Because earth-life is probationary in nature, the Lord has allowed the enemy a certain degree of freedom to influence, allure, oppose and even attack believers.

Although devils don't live outside the realm of Time as only the Lord does, they can still predict much of what will befall us in life. Through careful observation they know our areas of vulnerability. Demonic entities are laying in wait along the path of life.

The first thing they attempt to do with a believer is to influence his thinking. In the day in which we live, they primarily do this through the area of entertainment: *i.e.*, television, the internet, secular radio, etc. Whenever a Christian participates in such practices, he is allowing the enemy—through their godless followers—to shape his thinking.

Devils are also in the business of tempting believers into various forms of sin. An apt picture is a naïve young man strolling down a street in Tijuana. Along the way there are pitchmen whose sole occupation is luring unwary travelers into their seedy bars where they will be accosted by brazen prostitutes. Sexual sin is a fitting picture of someone being tempted into sin, but the truth is that the same spiritual transaction occurs with the person tempted to indulge in gossip, pride or any of a hundred other vices.

Also laying in ambush for the believer are demons whose primary purpose is to emotionally and even physically harm the person. This can occur by the biting tongue of a coworker, a humiliating experience, an illness or an injury of some sort. Satan and his minions are malevolent creatures whose sole satisfaction comes through causing others to suffer—especially the godly.

First and foremost, David had spiritual enemies, and he pleads with God to take up his cause in the spiritual realm. "Blow them away like chaff in the wind—wind sent by the Angel of the Lord," he pleads. "Make their path dark and slippery before them, with the Angel of the Lord pursuing them."

Every true believer has spiritual enemies as well. We too may ask the Lord to take up our cause and overcome the attacking enemy in our lives.

AND HOW ABOUT YOU?

- *Is there an area of your life that you feel vulnerable to the enemy's temptations?*

- *Is there anyone in your life the enemy uses to hurt you? Then begin to ask the Lord to destroy the works of the devil in your life.*

Week Two: SUNDAY

In the Lord's Care

"The steps of good men are directed by the Lord. He delights in each step they take. If they fall it isn't fatal, for the Lord holds them with his hand." (Psalm 37:23-24 LB)

For one more devotional, we will keep with the analogy of life's journey. At first glance it might seem that today's Scripture contradicts the warnings about the dangers the believer will encounter in this devil infested world we read about yesterday. And Scripture is very clear about the fact that even the elect can be deceived and led astray.

So what does David mean when he claims that even if "good men... fall, it isn't fatal?" The first thing that stands out is that this promise is made to "good men," those whose lives delight the Lord. Such marvelous promises are simply not made to half-hearted or worldly-minded Christians. Nominal (*i.e.,* "in name only") believers are very susceptible to being led astray through the way they live their lives. It is right that such people live in some degree of fear about the enemy's attempts to destroy them. They very well might fall—and fall fatally.

Bradley Furges, Director of Counseling at Pure Life Ministries, is fond of telling the men in our residential facility, "If you want to be kept, God will keep you." If a man makes decisions in his daily life that prove that he is uncommitted to the Lord, he has no right to expect God to keep him from heading back into a life of habitual sin.

However, if a person is sincerely trying to live a consecrated and obedient life, in other words, if his life is one in which the Lord would be delighted, then he has every right to expect the Lord to protect him from apostasy.

He will occasionally "fall," of course. The best of souls have hearts that are "prone to wander." Every believer fails at times. But, as someone once said, "Failure is not falling down, it is staying down."

Take Abraham, for instance. The Lord had told him to dwell in Canaan, but when a famine ravaged the land, he decided he needed to take the situation into his own hands and led his family down to Egypt. If it weren't for the Lord's merciful oversight in his life, he could have lost his beloved wife to the Pharaoh's harem. Yes, Abraham experienced a lapse in his trust in the Lord—a fall, if you will. But God was holding him by the hand. His grace covered his mistake and provided a way out of the crisis.

Every believer will make his mistakes, have his failures and even commit outright sins. But those who are sincerely doing their utmost to please the Lord in the way they conduct themselves in life, will find that He will be there when they fall, will pick them up and set them back on the right track.

AND HOW ABOUT YOU?

- *Do you share God's perspective on your failures, or do they tend to put you in a tailspin of despair?*
- *Has it been your experience that the Lord has been there to help you—even to the point of straightening out messes you have made— when you have "fallen?" That's a good sign! It means that you are headed in the right direction and God is caring for your soul.*

Notes

WEEK

THREE

The Horse and Mule

*"Do not be like the horse and the mule, senseless creatures
which will not come near you unless their spirit is tamed by
bit and bridle. Again and again the sinner must feel
the lash; he who trusts in the Lord finds nothing but
mercy all around him." (Psalm 32: 9-10 Knox)*

David paints a vivid picture of the carnal nature of man by alluding to these two "senseless creatures." Truly, those who are not under the influence and control of the Holy Spirit are utterly thickheaded to spiritual truths. (By contrast, Jesus said the Prodigal "came to his senses" in the pigpen and began the long journey back to his father.)

But these brute beasts' lack of sense is not the only spiritual reality that can be derived from this illustration. Although these two animals are similar in many ways, I believe David chose them to also illustrate their most distinguishing characteristics.

In its natural state, the horse is a wild and unruly animal. It is utterly useless to its human owner until it undergoes the long process of being broken of its own will. Here again we are presented with a perfect description of an unconquered man. He fights and bucks against all restraint being placed upon him. It is only after he has suffered long under the hand of sin's dominion that he will respond to the Master's loving invitation, "Come to me and I will give you rest—all of you who work so hard beneath a heavy yoke. Wear my yoke—for it fits perfectly—and let me teach you; for I am gentle and humble, and you shall find rest for your souls; for I give you only light burdens." (Matthew 11:28-30 LB)

Such a marvelous offer! Yet man is not quick to relinquish control over his own life. He truly is "stubborn as a mule." His natural response to the gospel message is to resist the conviction of the Holy Spirit, resist the God-given inclination to surrender and resist God's insistence on obedience.

Those who will not submit to the processes of God will eventually reap the consequences of their rebellion. The following translations accurately, if somewhat differently, convey the sense of verse 10:

- The sinner will be full of trouble... (BBE)
- An evil person suffers much pain... (NET)
- The torments of the wicked are many... (Har)

The Hebrew word translated "sinner" is a general term describing unbelievers. Those who will not subject themselves to God's authority, are certain to face a life of "much pain," many "torments" and "full of trouble." But this is also a relative spiritual truth. In other words, the degree to which a person is given over to rebellion will determine the sorrow he will face in life.

AND HOW ABOUT YOU?

- *Can you discern the difference between the normal hardships of life, the disciplines of the Lord and the consequences that come from rebellion?*

- *Do you regularly, consciously submit yourself to the Lord's yoke?*

The Desolated Soul

> *"The face of the LORD is against them that do evil, to cut off*
> *the remembrance of them from the earth. Evil shall slay the*
> *wicked: and they that hate the righteous shall be desolate."*
> *(Psalm 34:16, 21 KJV)*

Psalm 34 is a wonderful outpouring of love and gratitude penned by David after escaping from a dangerous situation with Philistines in Gath. For 22 verses he expresses one marvelous promise after another to those who love God. In the midst of this outpouring—and seemingly utterly out of place—he makes two statements about the wicked.

Perhaps he did so just to remind the godly what they have been spared in life. Whatever the case, David makes four assertions regarding those who will not obey God.

"Evil shall slay the wicked," he says. It sounds stark, as if the angel of death seized a person quickly and decisively—and, of course, there are times this actually occurs. Think about the many stories you have heard about famous sinners suffering violent deaths. But actually, I think David had in mind the slow working poison that destroys a person over time. The ungodly person becomes increasingly involved in sin and little by little he destroys his soul. "Those who live only to satisfy their own sinful nature," claims Paul, "will harvest decay and death from that sinful nature." (Galatians 6:8 NLT)

David also tells us, "The face of the LORD is against them that do evil." This could just as easily be translated, "The presence of the Lord..." as the Hebrew term can mean either. One can only imagine the implications of having God's wrath breaking out against someone's soul—continually, relentlessly, forever. As Spurgeon stated, "Hell itself is but evil fully developed, torturing those in whom it dwells."[1]

As if these dire warnings aren't enough to frighten the most stouthearted sinner, he continues by telling the reader that those who "hate the righteous shall be desolate." I don't believe he was limiting this punishment to those who detest and loathe believers. There are people like that, but I think the word "hate" here simply means that these wicked people are opposed to the kingdom of God and everyone associated with it.

Such people are undergoing a subtle and systematic process within their souls. They are being hollowed out, emptied of everything decent and worthy. While they are on this earth, where they can still reap the benefits of being in the environs of the godly people they despise, the disintegrating process is slowed down. But once they cross into the eternal realm, there will be nothing to hold back this process of spiritual decay.

Lastly, such people will have their memory "cut off" from the land of the living. Those who imagine others forever recalling fond memories of them are kidding themselves. People go on with life and, over time, all memories of the lost are gone.

AND HOW ABOUT YOU?

- *Have you thanked God lately for sparing you from these consequences of sin?*

- *Do you have unsaved loved ones? Perhaps these fearful warnings can serve as a catalyst for heartfelt pleadings on their behalf.*

Notes

When the Foundations are Shaken

"The foundations of law and order have collapsed.
What can the righteous do?" (Psalm 11:3 NLT)

These were the whining words of a coward. Yes, it is true, Psalms 11 and 12 tell of a time when society on the whole had turned bad. The friend of young David who uttered the words above had certainly rightly discerned "the spirit of the age" in which he lived. A heavy blanket of evil seemed to rest upon the land. "The god of lies (had become) enthroned in the national heart."² There was an acute shortage of truly godly men. Society seemed to have reached the last stage of corruption "when vileness is exalted" and "the wicked strut about on every side."

If this describes the social life a young David encountered 3,000 years ago, how much more is it true of the culture in which we live today? America has slipped far away from the decency that once established acceptable standards for our nation. Unquestionably, we live in a day when evil is reaching its climax. Many believers respond to this spiritual blight with the same defeatist attitude expressed by David's timid friend. "No matter how hard we try to live godly lives, the world around us only gets darker. It's hopeless to fight this losing battle! What can a righteous man do but bend to such times?"

What I would suggest is that the mindset represented with this sentiment is the very antithesis of righteousness. Solomon rightly said,

"Like a trampled spring and a polluted well is a righteous man who gives way before the wicked." (Proverbs 25:26)

The truth is that a righteous man would never express the faithless despair of David's friend. In other words, a righteous man wouldn't think to ask, "What can the righteous do?" He would ask, "What *cannot* the righteous do?" It is in the darkest part of the night that the stars shine their brightest. It is when evil is at its malignant peak that the deeds of the righteous stand out most clearly. Perhaps it is true that ordinary men acquiesce when "vileness is exalted," but just as true is that those of extra-ordinary faith rise to the occasion. Although godly men most keenly feel the pain of abounding wickedness, they are set apart by a dogged, stubborn unwillingness to bow to the evil of their times. Hebrews 11, the Book of Acts and the annals of Church history are chock-full of the stories of courageous men and women who, equipped with nothing more than faith in an almighty God, stood up to the evil of their times and made a difference.

In the dark days in which we live, let us each stand for righteousness and fight for the souls of the lost around us.

And how about you?

- *As we see the moral fabric of our culture frazzling before our eyes, are you sometimes tempted to "hide your light under a bushel?"*

- *What is God calling you to do to hinder and slow down the progress of evil?*

Week Three: THURSDAY

The Death of Piety

"Lord, come to my rescue; piety is dead; in a base world,
true hearts have grown rare." (Psalm 12:1 Knox)

" **C**ritical mass" is a term sociologists have borrowed from nuclear scientists to describe the phenomenon within a culture when a certain idea is championed by a few and eventually adopted by the majority. As we saw yesterday, Psalms 11 and 12 describe a period when society on the whole had taken on an evil flavor. The momentum had gradually shifted from prevailing decency to widespread corruption.

"When vileness is exalted," one of the features of human interaction that is most affected is speech. David said that in such times, "They speak vanity every one with his neighbor: with flattering lips and with a double heart do they speak... the tongue that speaketh proud things." (Psalm 12:2-3 KJV)

Most translations use the term "falsehood" in place of "vanity" in this sentence. Both are correct. This word (Heb. *shâv*) is used to describe "vain idols" (Psalm 31:6) and "deceitful men" (Psalm 26:4). In either case, the sense of the term is that it describes something that is void of reality; when describing speech, the point is that people are using words that are empty of truth. David is here describing a time that had become so corrupted that "this spirit of falsehood infested their most intimate relations."[3] Dishonesty and fraudulence had become so entrenched in the culture that David lamented finding any honest souls.

The time of which David referred was also one where flattery abounded. Of course, a person flatters another—exaggerates the person's qualities or talents—for his own selfish purposes. He lavishes the person with praise because he knows it is the quickest way into the person's good graces. Influential people are continually subjected to flatterers who wish to use them for their own advancement.

Such people not only flatter others, but they flatter themselves. They love to talk glowingly about their talents and accomplishments. They speak "proud things" and are quick to "name-drop" to prove their value. Times are indeed bad when such fawning, morally-bankrupt people worm their way into positions of influence.

What distresses me is to see the evangelical community infected with this same spirit. The Church is in trouble when its leaders flatter their audiences rather than telling them the truth about their spiritual condition; when liars, flatterers and prideful preachers use their smooth speech to gain influence among God's people; when man is exalted rather than Christ. They are "perilous times" indeed when the Church is overrun with such charlatans.

Whatever might be the moral climate of our generation, we must stand firm in the Truth; we must be honest about our spiritual condition, avoid all forms of flattery and prideful talk. Only then can we stand as lights within an evil generation.

AND HOW ABOUT YOU?

• *Do you ever witness this kind of falsehood in the Church?*

• *Do you ever engage in flattery yourself?*

• *We must pray that the Lord will weed out the false teachers in our midst. We must also pray that the Lord will help us to keep our own hearts honest and upright even when there is a temptation to use flattering words to gain someone's approval.*

The Poisoned Mind

> *"O Lord...preserve me from the violent, who plot and stir*
> *up trouble all day long. Their words sting like poisonous*
> *snakes. Keep me out of their power. Preserve me from*
> *their violence, for they are plotting against me."*
> *(Psalm 140:1-4 LB)*

Unquestionably, Satan and his fallen followers are like cunning serpents. In the spiritual realm—that mysterious, unseen world which coincides with ours—they have the power to infect the minds of humans.

Of course, it goes without saying that they have free reign over the hearts and minds of the ungodly. Those who continue to live in rebellion to God's authority have no protection whatsoever from their influence. Such people are still residing in the kingdom of darkness so it only makes sense that they would be fully tuned in to the voice of darkness. Satan is the god of this world: their chosen deity. Unless they repent, they will live out their entire existence on earth under his sway. They will take his mindset with them on into their eternal home.

The situation for pseudo-Christians is slightly different. They too live fully under the control of the enemy. In their case, they have been deceived into believing that they are living in God's kingdom. They have willingly bought the lie that they can be one person inside and another outwardly. "They profess to know God, but by their deeds they deny *Him*…" (Titus 1:16) They are every bit as lost and a part of Satan's kingdom as the heathen.

For the most part believers live under divine protection from the enemy's assaults. I say "for the most part" because we do still have a free will, and when we willingly enter the enemy's camp we open ourselves up to his influence. For instance, if a Christian man goes into a pornographic website, he cannot expect God to protect him from the lurid thoughts that will continually plague him in the months to come. Another example of this—albeit less dramatic—is television. When believers watch secular television, they are opening themselves up to the enemy's malicious input.

However, innocent Christians are also susceptible to the enemy's suggestions. True, the enemy can go no further than God allows, but earth is a testing ground and the Lord does allow His children to undergo trials.

One example of how demons inject their poison into the minds of believers is in their interrelations with other people. It is amazing how vulnerable we can be to evil suggestions about other people. We are taught that love "is ever ready to believe the best of every person" (1 Corinthians 13:7 Amp) and that "love covers a multitude of sins." (1 Peter 4:8) Yet it is amazing how readily we believe the evil report about others.

Sometimes it comes to us through the tongues of others. Gossip and slander are two of the enemy's greatest tools. Demons have been successfully destroying relationships and splitting churches with these simple techniques for thousands of years.

But the enemy can also breathe his poisonous thoughts into our minds. One foul suggestion can powerfully distort a person's perspective about another. Once that thinking has taken hold of his mind, everything the other person does or says is viewed through this distorted lens. We are still susceptible to such mental impressions because we still have a fallen nature.

That being the case, the psalmist's prayer is a good one to use: "Lord, their words sting like poisonous snakes. Keep me out of their power."

AND HOW ABOUT YOU?

- *Are you ever plagued with negative thoughts about a loved one or a coworker?*

- *Do you fight against these thoughts or have you been in the habit of indulging them? Perhaps you can now look "beyond the veil" and see the enemy's involvement.*

- *Why not make David's prayer your own?*

Notes

Divine Interruption

> *"Because his love is set on me, I will deliver him; I will*
> *lift him beyond danger, for he knows me by my name.*
> *When he calls upon me, I will answer; I will be with*
> *him in time of trouble; I will rescue him and bring him*
> *to honor. I will satisfy him with long life to enjoy the*
> *fullness of my salvation." (Psalm 91:14-16 NEB)*

Psalm 91 contains two separate conditional promises. The psalmist begins by describing a person who sees God as his provider and protector. Most translations offer the more literal sense of a person living under God's shelter, but R.K. Harrison beautifully captured the essence of what was being stated when he wrote: "He who lives as a ward of the Most High..." (Psalm 91:1 Har)

The picture Harrison paints is that of an orphan who places himself in the custody of the State. He understands that if he will abide by the designated rules all his basic needs will be provided.

Furthermore, the psalmist says the person who puts himself in Jehovah's care will be afforded overwhelming protection. He goes on, in the next dozen verses, to list some fifteen different ways God will keep and defend His beloved. Then, just as he seems to get on a roll with his thoughts, God suddenly stops him, as it were, takes over the conversation and offers His own conditional promise—separate from but in addition to what the psalmist was offering.

These two sections of the psalm speak to me of two different types of believers. In the first section of this psalm, the psalmist seems to refer to the person who has entered into a place of saving faith. This is not describing a false professor—someone who merely talks the talk—but a person who truly puts his life in the hands of the Almighty. He has committed himself to living as a "ward of the State," so to speak. He understands that if he will abide by the rules he will be entitled to receive the promised benefits.

The Lord seems to have something greater in mind, though.

It is as if the Lord is saying, "Listen, that's not the half of it! If he will truly love Me, if he will really enter into an intimate relationship with Me, if he will give his entire heart to me, yes, yes, I will keep him out of spiritual danger, but I will do so much more for him! I will abundantly answer every prayer he utters. I will honor him in a way that others will know that he is my friend. And, if all of that isn't enough, I will give him a rich and fulfilling life—one that he will enjoy forever!"

If we will but trust in the Lord, we are promised to be cared for; but if we will go beyond that childish level and step up into the realm of friendship with God, He will overwhelm us with the richest blessings He has to offer!

AND HOW ABOUT YOU?

- *Where do you see yourself in this psalm?*

- *Have you experienced God's paternal care for your soul?*

- *Can you see yourself as His personal "ward?"*

- *Have you moved beyond that level into true friendship with Him? If you have, surely you know what it means to be lavished with His love!*

Divine Promises

> *"Because his love is set on me, I will deliver him; I will*
> *lift him beyond danger, for he knows me by my name.*
> *When he calls upon me, I will answer; I will be with*
> *him in time of trouble; I will rescue him and bring him*
> *to honor. I will satisfy him with long life to enjoy the*
> *fullness of my salvation." (Psalm 91:14-16 NEB)*

Yesterday we observed the psalmist sharing two sets of promises—divine protection for those who believed in the Lord and divine blessings for those who truly set their hearts on Him. Today I want to explore those promises a little more deeply.

The person to whom these promises have been made has given the Lord the deepest affections his heart has to share. When he says, "I love the Lord," one can sense that those words are not spoken as a trite phrase he has learned from others; he clearly means what he says. When God looks upon his inward life, what He sees—with much gratification—is someone who loves Him with all his heart, soul and mind.

It is after this spiritual/emotional transaction has occurred that we are told that he knows the Lord by name. One would expect the order to be reversed, but actually we will never truly know God until we have given our hearts to Him completely. This person has entered into intimate fellowship with God.

As for the promises, I want to focus on the last two.

The Lord promises honor to this person. Does that mean that He will arrange circumstances such as He did for Mordecai when he was led through the city on a horse, while Haman proclaimed to all the on-looking crowds that he was favored by the king? No, probably not.

While the word honor (Heb. *kebed*) literally means "to be heavy," it is rarely employed in that context. It is almost always used in Scripture regarding someone's character. So, in essence, to the one who sincerely loves Him, the Lord is promising to add weighty substance to his character. It isn't that he will be paraded through the streets or given a mega-ministry; it means that the Lord will transform him into a person people instinctively know is a noble man.

The other promise I want to touch on is the last sentence of this psalm: "I will satisfy him with long life to enjoy the fullness of my salvation." In the Old Testament period, "long life" was a phrase that primarily described a full life—or, as was said of David and Job, "full of days."

In other words, their lives were rich in God's blessing and they died fully satisfied. When they were lying on their death bed, they weren't frantically grasping for another day on earth. No, for many years they had experienced God's goodness and now they were ready to depart. There was no reluctance to face eternity but a bright hope. Life had been good to them and they were ready to cross the River into the city of God.

Such is the ending to the person's life who has given his heart to God. When loved ones gather around his casket, the preacher will not be struggling to find something nice to say. He will be able to exclaim, "This was a good man who loved his God. He died happy and content. He had experienced God's goodness in the land of the living.

AND HOW ABOUT YOU?

- *I suppose to love the Lord with all one's inner life means that all competing loves have been swallowed up in one great passion for God. Does that describe your heart or do you detect competing desires lurking within?*

WEEK

FOUR

Lurking Sins

"But how can I know what sins are lurking in my heart?
Cleanse me from these hidden faults." (Psalm 19:12 LB)

Seasoned spelunkers understand something that you and I only know vaguely: there is an entire culture of creatures that live in the vast world of underground caves. Centipedes, bats and snakes are but a few of the inhabitants of these lower regions.

Humans also have an outward, observable life as well as an unseen realm known mostly only by themselves. Elsewhere David said that "the inward thought and the heart of a man are deep." (Psalm 64:6) The depraved nature and diseased soul make this inner realm the perfect habitat for the foulest of creatures: selfishness, pride, greed, envy, hatred, perversion and so on.

Once the light of God's Word illuminates this dark region, the new believer is now confronted with the reality of his fallen nature. No wonder Paul exclaimed: "I love to do God's will so far as my new nature is concerned; but there is something else deep within me, in my lower nature, that is at war with my mind and wins the fight and makes me a slave to the sin that is still within me..." (Romans 7:22-23 LB)

Notwithstanding this dual nature, we must remember that God created humans with a conscience—the moral compass of the soul. It oversees every street and alley of a person's inside world. The problem is that it is part of the flawed system it seeks to monitor. It is like a corrupt cop who has been bribed by local gangsters to look the other way when they do their dirty work.

The Lord's answer to this dilemma is the Word of God: the honest "cop" who has the ability to ferret out and expose every false and decrepit intruder lurking in the human soul. "For the Word that God speaks is alive and full of power [*making it active, operative, energizing, and effective*]; it is sharper than any two-edged sword, penetrating to the dividing line of the breath of life (soul) and [*the immortal*] spirit, and of joints and marrow [*of the deepest parts of our nature*], exposing and sifting and analyzing and judging the very thoughts and purposes of the heart." (Hebrews 4:12 Amp)

Yes, there is a vast system lying within us which harbors a mass of black sin. But the Holy Spirit will use God's Word to cleanse the inner life of any sincere believer who invites His sanctifying work. Let us join with David in the prayer, "O God, let the secrets of my heart be uncovered…" (Psalm 139:23 BBE) "Cleanse me from these hidden faults."

And how about you?

- *Is the Lord bringing to mind any sin that has been lurking in your heart?*

- *Do you actively seek God's sanctifying work inside you, or do you do your best to avoid and ignore the Holy Spirit's inner promptings? If you pray David's prayer, the Lord will faithfully answer.*

An Emphatic Plea

> *"Have mercy upon me, O God, according to thy*
> *lovingkindness: according unto the multitude of thy tender*
> *mercies blot out my transgressions. Wash me thoroughly from*
> *mine iniquity, and cleanse me from my sin. For I acknowledge*
> *my transgressions: and my sin is ever before me."*
> *(Psalm 51:1-3 KJV)*

The verses above represent one of the most dramatic changes of heart ever recorded. It had been about a year since David's shameful deeds with Bathsheba and her husband had occurred. For months he had languished in spiritual deadness until Nathan finally confronted him. (2 Samuel 12) But the instant he saw the reality of his condition, all his internal resistance to the Holy Spirit's conviction collapsed. He immediately acknowledged his sin and spent a week fasting and praying.*

There are a number of features to this prayer that provide valuable lessons for all of us redeemed sinners.

The first thing that stands out is that David did nothing to minimize his sins. He knew his actions were deplorable and took full responsibility for them. He didn't attempt to blame childhood trauma, Bathsheba's ill-advised bathing or even the devil for leading him into such a place of temptation. He fully understood that his was a "deep and dreadful guilt" and that any attempt to justify himself now would thwart God's ability to break the power of sin in his heart.

---

* Part of the motivation for his prayer and fasting was the death sentence hanging over his baby. (2 Samuel 12:14-18)

Another noticeable thing about his prayer is how he appeals to God's long history of merciful dealings with other sinners in similar situations. "According unto the multitude of thy tender mercies blot out my transgressions," he prayed. With the Lord's smiling approval, David points at God's mercy to penitents as a precedent for his situation.

The middle-aged king was also very aware that every one of his deplorable actions during that shameful year was recorded in the annals of heaven. A perfectly accurate account has been taken of his behavior. "Please Lord, erase the record of my sinful deeds! Expunge the record of my crimes!"

Many sinners would stop there, content to receive a pardon, even though the sin continued to fester within their hearts. But David desired more for himself than mere forgiveness. He looked within and saw a black mass of corruption entwined around his heart—almost as if he could see the putrefying effects of leprosy there. He wanted to be cleansed of every contaminated spot remaining within.

The level of passion in his repentance can be seen in the verbs he employed throughout this psalm: *blot out, wash me thoroughly, cleanse me, purify me, create in me, renew, do not cast me away, restore, sustain* and so on. It is as if the words burst forth from the deepest parts of his being.

The kind of repentance that allows God to break the power of sin within one's heart requires total sincerity, abject humility, absolute honesty and a willingness to accept the Lord's discipline—no matter what it might be. This is why David was set free that week and why so many in our day remain bogged down in habitual sin.

AND HOW ABOUT YOU?

- *What has your repentance been like?*
- *Do you have a long track record of ongoing repentance, or was it a single act that occurred long ago?*
- *Do you honestly want God to purge the sin out of your heart?*

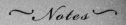

~Notes~

~Notes~

Thoroughly Wretched

*"But I was born a sinner, yes, from the moment my mother
conceived me. You deserve honesty from the heart; yes,
utter sincerity and truthfulness. Oh, give me this wisdom."*
(Psalm 51:5-6 LB)

In today's devotional, we are cutting into the middle of David's sincere confession and repentance concerning his sinful actions with Bathsheba. After thoroughly acknowledging his guilt and casting himself upon God's mercy, he now seems to take a slight detour with two astounding discoveries.

The first thing David realizes is that he can trace his sinful condition all the way back to his birth. Although he inherited this spiritual disease, he does not attempt to justify his actions. He also does not try to spin some theological theory about his behavior. Alexander MacLaren writes: "He does not think that sin is the less his, because the tendency has been inherited. But he is spreading all his condition before God. In fact, he is not so much thinking of his criminality as of his desperate need. From a burden so heavy and so entwined with himself none but God can deliver him. He cannot cleanse himself, for self is infected. He cannot find cleansing among men, for they too have inherited the poison."[1]

On the heels of this startling discovery he looks within and finds that his entire inward being is polluted. He knows that during the past year he has been dishonest with himself. He has avoided the truth about his affair with Bathsheba. It is time to face the truth about himself—no matter what the consequences might be.

ENTERING HIS COURTS

Charles Spurgeon states: "Reality, sincerity, true holiness, heart-fidelity, these are the demands of God. He cares not for the pretence of purity, he looks to the mind, heart, and soul. Always has the Holy One of Israel estimated men by their inner nature, and not by their outward professions; to him the inward is as visible as the outward, and he rightly judges that the essential character of an action lies in the motive of him who works it."[2]

This segment of David's penitential prayer is not the rationalization of a hypocrite. It is also not the sinner who accuses God of being too demanding. It is the sincere cry of a man who sees that he is in deep trouble. And yet, at the same time, it is a prayer that is full of faith. He has complete assurance in the fact that if he is sincere with the Lord, he will be forgiven and cleansed of the contamination of his sin.

Every true believer has, at some time in his life, come to grips with his sinful condition. This realization can be very upsetting. Nevertheless, the sincere person will look over the long history of his life and come to God with a heartfelt sorrow over, not only his sinful actions but the sinful disposition that produced them. Then, with faith in God's merciful character, he will look for the assurance of the pardon that is sure to come.

AND HOW ABOUT YOU?

- *Have you come to grips with your sinful nature?*
- *Has this awareness provoked a subtle attitude of complacency, or a greater determination to seek God's aid in changing you?*

Week Four: THURSDAY

Create In Me a Clean Heart

"Create in me a clean heart, O God, and renew
a steadfast spirit within me. Do not cast me away
from Your presence and do not take Your Holy Spirit
from me." (Psalm 51:10-11)

David has been pouring his heart out in penitential prayer.
Having accepted by faith the forgiveness and inner cleansing
he desperately needed, he now begins to consider his future relationship
with God. He accomplishes this with four distinct words that conjure up
meaningful pictures from the past.

He begins this section of the prayer with the words, "Create in
me a clean heart." The word create (Heb. *berâ'*) is the same word used
to describe the world's formation in Genesis 1:1. David understood
that he needed something brand new to take the place of the old,
fallen nature that had so readily given in to temptation. This petition
is an anticipation of what God would promise His people through the
prophets: "Moreover, I will give you a new heart and put a new spirit
within you; and I will remove the heart of stone from your flesh and
give you a heart of flesh." (Ezekiel 36:26) This would ultimately be possible
only through the shed blood of Christ on Calvary.

The second term he utilized was "renew." This word has in mind
rebuilding something that was once in existence. The literal usage of
it can be found in 2 Chronicles 24:4 where Ezra wrote, "Now it came

about after this that Joash decided to *restore* the house of the LORD." David sees that the spirit which had once served God faithfully had been shattered through neglect. He implores the Lord to rebuild it.

The next phrase ("Do not cast me away…") at once brings to mind the terrible picture of Cain. After receiving God's judicial sentence, he cries out in anguish, "My punishment is too great to bear! Behold… from Your face I will be hidden." (Genesis 4:13-14) David cannot bear the thought of being banished from the Lord's presence, but he knows that is what he deserves.

The last picture presented ("…do not take Your Holy Spirit from me.") was one that David personally witnessed. It was actually on the occasion of David's anointing by Samuel that this happened to Saul. "Then… the Spirit of the LORD came mightily upon David from that day forward. And… the Spirit of the LORD departed from Saul, and an evil spirit from the LORD terrorized him." (1 Samuel 16:13-14) David probably shuddered to think of the internal anguish that marked the old king's final days.

Whether or not all of these pictures were in David's mind when he penned these words, they certainly bring to light the sense behind these four terms. Even if we have not committed horrendous sins, these four phrases offer meaningful prayers to keep in our arsenal.

AND HOW ABOUT YOU?

• *Have you seen your own wretchedness?*

• *Can you relate to these four phrases of David's prayer? If you can, perhaps this would be an appropriate prayer for you to keep in your arsenal: "Lord, keep my heart clean and my spirit strong. Keep me close to Your presence and let Your Spirit thrive within me."*

• *Has there been a "Nathan" in your life who confronted you at some point? Have you even thanked this person?*

Week Four: FRIDAY

Beyond Offerings

*"You don't want penance; if you did, how gladly I would
do it! You aren't interested in offerings burned before you
on the altar. It is a broken spirit you want—remorse and
penitence. A broken and a contrite heart, O God,
you will not ignore." (Psalm 51:16-17 LB)*

To the biblical student, this portion of David's penitential prayer might seem out of order. The Mosaic Law prescribed in great detail what was required of a sinner desiring forgiveness. He was to bring the designated animal to the Temple altar where it was to be sacrificed as an atonement for his sins. It is not for man to decide how he will approach the Almighty in his search for pardon. Yet, how many in our current church culture contrive their own path to forgiveness? Such people have an entitlement attitude toward God; that He somehow owes them forgiveness.

The purpose of the great sacrificial system inaugurated by Moses was to impress upon the sinner the gravity of his transgressions. He was required to slit the throat of that spotless lamb so that he could sense the weight of his iniquity. It was meant to leave the man with an impression that he would not soon forget.

Yet, there is nothing in David's prayer that gives the slightest sense that he was attempting to avoid the consequences of his crimes or attempting to approach God on his own terms. In fact, one gets the sense that he would have gladly offered 1,000 sheep or bullocks on that altar if he felt it would appease the God he had offended.

But David was not satisfied with performing an outward ritual. He probably had seen insincere sacrifices made at that altar many times. As one minister wrote, "A man may offer bodily sacrifice, and perform outward duties to God, and yet stand aloof from Him, and have his heart still reserved to himself."[3] Another wrote, "The bullocks that are to be sacrificed now are our hearts; it were easier for me to give him bullocks for sacrifice, than to give him my heart."[4]

In our day and age, we don't make sacrifices; we have developed a prescribed prayer formula that has taken the place of the old sacrificial system. One can only imagine the countless times the Lord has been forced to endure prayers of repentance from insincere people.

David was getting at the heart of the issue of atonement. He knew that the sacrificial system was meant to bring a person into a deeper sense of guilt and shame over his sin. The Lord was not looking for the outward forms of penitence but the true contrition of heart that is always evident in sincere repentance.

Such signs of brokenness God would never "ignore," or, as other translations say, "despise." But what is thoroughly appreciated by God is disdained by man. Humble people have always been held in contempt by the proud—whether they are brazen sinners or professing believers.

A hard heart is a heart of stone. It lacks the suppleness of the one who is in a place of brokenness. Such people might keep the outward semblances of religion, but God sees their callousness, stubbornness and pride.

And how about you?

- *Have you ever entertained an entitlement attitude in your heart regarding past or present sins?*

- *Or have you truly experienced the kind of godly sorrow over sins that has broken your heart?*

Notes

The Purpose of Brokenness

> *"God's sacrifice is a soul with its evil crushed;*
> *a heart broken with penitence, O God, never*
> *wilt thou despise." (Psalm 51:17 Mof)*

The placement of this verse in David's prayer is significant. One would have expected such statements to come on the heels of his earlier statements of contrition found in the first four verses. It would make sense to hear about "the joy of salvation" (vs. 12), teaching transgressors the ways of God (vs. 13) and joyfully singing about God's righteousness (vs. 14) *after* all the business of repentance had been dispensed with.

But if there is one thing that stands out throughout this psalm it is that David is thinking about the long term aspects of his relationship with the Lord. When he asks to be thoroughly cleansed of his iniquity (vs. 2), purified with hyssop (vs. 7), given a steadfast spirit (vs. 10) and promises to teach transgressors (vs. 13), he is showing that he is making a long term commitment to remain faithful to God.

Many people offer up a superficial prayer of repentance and cannot seem to "move on" quickly enough. It is as if they want to put as much distance as possible between themselves and the sense of brokenness and humility they have just experienced. But what is the point of repentance if it doesn't accomplish the kind of heart change that will prevent the sins from happening again?

Repentance was never meant to be a one act show; it is supposed to be a regular facet of the new life one has entered into. The truth is that sincere believers are never very far from tears. How can they be, when every time they look within, they see the depravity of their own natures?

In the first four verses of Psalm 51, David thoroughly repented of the sins he had committed. I'm sure that if he would have stopped there God would have still been very pleased with the sincerity and intensity of his penitence. But David no sooner begins to feel the relief of the burden of guilt and the joy of his salvation, then he returns to his penitential posture. In other words, he saw brokenness over his sinful nature as something that would become an integral part of his future life.

And how about you?

- *Can you see the tendency to move quickly past repentance in your own life?*
- *Has repentance remained a vital part of your spiritual life? If not, ask the Lord to bring you to a greater awareness of your need for ongoing repentance.*

The Ears of the Heart

"My heart has heard you say, "Come and talk with
me." And my heart responds, "Lord, I am coming."
(Psalm 27:8 NLT)

According to the apostle Paul, the human being possesses "eyes of the heart." (Ephesians 1:18) I assume that this expression was coined to express the fact that a believer has the capacity to see things in the spiritual realm which cannot be seen with physical eyesight.

In a similar way, people have "ears of the heart." In the great vision Isaiah had of the Lord on His throne, we can see an example of spiritual eyes and ears. He said to the prophet, "Go, and tell this people: Keep on listening, but do not perceive; keep on looking, but do not understand. Render the hearts of this people insensitive, their ears dull, and their eyes dim, otherwise they might see with their eyes, hear with their ears, understand with their hearts, and return and be healed." (Isaiah 6:9-10) It isn't a person's physical eyes and ears that can perceive the things of the spiritual realm but the heart.

In one of His discourses, Jesus referred to Himself as the shepherd of His people, and said that "the sheep hear his voice, and he calls his own sheep by name and leads them out." (John 10:3) He is clearly referring to the call to follow Him. Here, too, we see an example of those who have spiritual ears.

In our subject verse above, David claims that his heart has heard the Lord calling to him. His answer is that he hears the call and is responding to it. Seeking the Lord is one of the great principles of the Christian faith. Believers should do their utmost to strive to press in spiritually: to ask for, to plead for, even to beg for the presence of God. This should be an ongoing discipline of the Christian life and yet there are certain occasions when the Lord makes His follower to know that he would be richly blessed if he would seek His face *right now*.

There is a Greek term *(kairos)* that is sometimes translated as "time," while on other occasions the word "opportunity" is the chosen English word. The spiritual meaning of this term is that there are certain occasions in life when a spiritual opportunity presents itself and it is wise to take advantage of it. I believe that is the sense of what is being expressed in Psalm 27:8.

The Lord has moved near to David, is calling him to seek His face, to press into His presence. The poet/king understands that this is one of those precious moments when he can derive much good for his soul if he will take advantage of the opportunity.

AND HOW ABOUT YOU?

- *Do you have "ears to hear" when the Lord beckons you to seek His face?*
- *Are you aware of anything that may be dulling your hearing?*
- *Are you quick to respond when you hear that "still, small voice?" Perhaps it would be good to ask the Lord to open the ears of your heart that you might better hear His call when it comes.*

WEEK

FIVE

Fleeting Phantoms

> *"Man is a mere phantom as he goes to and fro: He bustles about, but only in vain; he heaps up wealth, not knowing who will get it. But now, Lord, what do I look for? My hope is in you."* (Psalm 39:6-7 NIV)

In this short passage David sums up the human existence on earth in its entirety. But the colorful language he employs makes it a very profound perspective on man's great eternal question.

Before we look at the picture he has drawn for us, let's take a quick look at a couple of these terms. The NIV translates the Hebrew word *tselem* as "phantom." It is an apt English word to utilize here. Albert Barnes says, "the idea seems to be that of an image, as contradistinguished from a reality; the shadow of a thing, as distinguished from the substance."[1]

The other term we should glance at is "bustles," (Heb. *hâmâh*) which is used to describe the disturbance within a soul, the roaring of the waves and the commotion of a riot. Consider other translations of this sentence:

- Surely every man walks to and fro—like a shadow in a pantomime; surely for futility and emptiness he is in turmoil.(AMP)

- We are merely moving shadows, and all our busy rushing ends in nothing. (NLT)

- Mere phantoms, we go our way; mere vapor, our restless pursuits. (NAB)

So David here pictures unredeemed man, rushing about in a frantic uproar in the pursuit of empty possessions and vain experiences; in short, a life which is far below the nobility for which he was created.

The picture I have in my mind of man is that he begins life in a neutral position in some sense. The way he lives his life over the next 70 years or so will determine the substance of his life. He is, as it were, either adding substance to or depleting his eternal being.

If we are living for this temporal earth life, with all of its glittering toys and pleasurable experiences, we are only making ourselves increasingly empty. But, if it is the Lord for whom we are searching and upon whom we have attached life's hopes, we will become increasingly more substantial.

When God surveys our lives, is He seeing nothing more than ghosts, phantoms, fleeting here and there in the pursuit of more temporal vanity? Or is He seeing valuable lives lived out by people of character and substance?

The truth is that very few people can resist the natural tendency to see the shadows of life as being the true reality, and the substance of the spiritual realm as the fairytale. It is the very vanity of earth life that explains the hollow satisfaction it offers and it is the very substantial nature of our life in God that explains the sense of fulfillment it provides.

And how about you?

- *Where do you gain your sense of fulfillment in life?*

- *What are the true treasures of your heart?*

- *Do you see your life on earth as an opportunity to glorify God, or as an opportunity to gratify your lower nature?*

Week Five: TUESDAY

Limited Blessings

*"Oh, how often they rebelled against him in those
desert years and grieved his heart. Again and again
they... limited the Holy One of Israel from giving
them his blessings." (Psalm 78:40-41 LB)*

What a bountiful heart lies within the bosom of our Heavenly Father! I suspect that one of His greatest pleasures is to bless His children with "good things." How sad it is that we so often thwart His kind intentions to bestow such blessings.

God's perspective in this relationship became real to me one time when I found myself in a situation where I was the one giving to another person. There was a particular Christian who I cared about very much. A certain set of circumstances unfolded in such a way that I was going to be in the position to do something very special for this person. However, it was going to take several weeks to accomplish it.

My excitement mounted as I looked to the day I would be able to present my gift. About two weeks before the grand announcement, I received some very disturbing news from a reliable source. The beneficiary of my small act of kindness had done something extremely selfish, deeply hurting another loved one. In one instant, the bottom fell out of my excitement. I still loved this person, but the last thing I wanted to do at that moment was to go through with my surprise gift. The whole plan had already been set in motion and I did in fact make my presentation.

Unfortunately, it proved to be a very hollow experience for me.

I can't help but wonder how many times the Lord has longed to pour out blessings upon His children, but our selfish actions have hindered Him. I suppose only eternity will tell the full story of how often we have cheated ourselves of God's rich bounty.

Yes, there are those occasions when the Lord goes through with His intended gifts—even though our behavior has not warranted such blessings. At the very least our selfishness has robbed Him of the joy of blessing us—grieved His heart, in fact.

Then there are those times when He gives us what we demand, even though consequences will surely accompany it. Psalm 78 tells the story of the children of Israel in the wilderness demanding food from God. The Message offers it in modern vernacular: "They whined like spoiled children, 'Why can't God give us a decent meal in this desert? Sure, he struck the rock and the water flowed, creeks cascaded from the rock. But how about some fresh-baked bread? How about a nice cut of meat?' When God heard that, he was furious—his anger flared against Jacob, he lost his temper with Israel." (Psalm 78:19-21 MSG)

Toying with God's giving nature certainly has its dangers. The best course of action is to live to please the Lord and allow Him to bless us as He sees fit. Surely He will be extremely generous if we will live our lives in this way.

AND HOW ABOUT YOU?

- *Have you ever considered how your actions affect God's propensity to bless you?*
- *Have you ever had to suffer the consequences of demanding something of the Lord that you knew was not pleasing to Him? Let us live to please Him and trust Him to bless us in His own good time!*

Notes

Jesus the Seeker

"The impious fool says in his heart, "There is no God."
How vile men are, how depraved and loathsome; not one
does anything good! The Lord looks down from heaven on
all mankind to see if any act wisely, if any seek out God.
But all are disloyal, all are rotten to the core; not one does
anything good, no, not even one." (Psalm 14:1-3 NEB)

The picture David presents to the reader is the divine Being conducting a systematic and comprehensive search around the world. Perhaps it is an allusion to "the seven Spirits of God, sent out into all the earth" (Revelation 5:6), or "the eyes of the LORD which range to and fro throughout the earth." (Zechariah 4:10) Whatever the case may be, it is clear that the Lord is leaving no stone unturned in His quest to find someone, anyone, who has an interest in personally knowing Him.

What a sad indictment on mankind that for all His looking, the Lord has not been able to find a single person who wanted Him. The truth is that the deeper His inspection went, the worse the news. His investigation of the human race discovers a couple of troubling facts.

First, the person mentioned here is representative of the entire human race. The translators were correct in labeling this person an "impious fool" because, biblically speaking, folly is always associated with sinfulness. But we must be careful not to think of this as only applying to blatant sinners. David quickly corrects any such notion with the next sentence: "not one does anything good!" And just to make sure there is no mistaking what he is saying, he repeats it in even stronger terms in the last sentence: "no, not even one."

The clear implication is that this describes the universal condition of the human race. "For all have sinned and fall short of the glory of God," Paul later added. (Romans 3:23)

Not only is the Lord's conclusion about mankind pervasive in its extent, it is also thorough in its depth.

The Lord is pictured as going right into man's heart—the very core of his being—to discover what makes him tick. It is there that He finds that man has considered the existence of God and has arrived at the insane conclusion that "there is no God."

The reason he has developed this conviction only makes the matter worse: He doesn't want to acknowledge a supreme Being because he doesn't want to answer to Him for his actions. He is inherently selfish and desires experiences which God has forbidden.

What hope does fallen man have? His hope is not in himself but in the Seeker of lost souls. Jesus described Himself as a shepherd who had lost one of his sheep and goes searching until he finds it. And when He does—here is the picture of God's loving heart—"he calls together his friends and his neighbors, saying to them, 'Rejoice with me, for I have found my sheep which was lost!'" (Luke 15:6)

What can we do but fall on our faces in utter gratitude?

And how about you?

- *Have you ever seriously contemplated the great work of salvation that God undertook to win your heart over to Himself?*

- *Have you considered the fact that there was nothing—nothing—in yourself that would attract His affection? Perhaps this would be an opportune time to reflect on these great truths and express to God the appropriate gratitude.*

Week Five: THURSDAY

Unmerciful Prayers

> *"O my God, save me from my enemies. Protect me from these who have come to destroy me... stagger them with your power and bring them to their knees. Bring them to the dust, O Lord our shield. They are proud, cursing liars. Angrily destroy them. Wipe them out. (And let the nations find out, too, that God rules in Israel and will reign throughout the world.)" (Psalm 59:1, 11-13 LB)*

Frankly, there are times when it is difficult to reconcile in my mind that the man who wrote the angry prayer above was the "sweet psalmist of Israel." Some of the words he wrote elsewhere were so full of love for God and compassion for the needy that we have to remind ourselves that he was also the same man who carried around the severed head of one of his vanquished foes.

But there is a deeper meaning in the "Imprecatory Psalms" than the petty vindictiveness they seem to convey.

God's grace and love were not fully revealed until Christ came to this earth. In David's day, the greatest need in the world was to get a sight of God's holy character. This godly man did not desire divine retribution simply for the sake of vengeance, but so that the pagan nations surrounding Israel would come to realize "that God rules in Israel and will reign throughout the world." People needed to know—and in that day and age it was best communicated through a show of force—that the God of Israel was almighty.

David's hope was that the judgment of openly wicked men would solicit an interest in knowing more about this powerful Deity. Israel was supposed to be a beacon of Light to a world entrapped in spiritual darkness. In his mind, he believed that this sort of judgment would awaken people to the reality of Jehovah.

In the previous psalm, David offered another purpose in the death of the ungodly. He wrote, "The godly shall... walk the blood-stained fields of slaughtered, wicked men. Then at last everyone will know that good is rewarded, and that there is a God who judges justly here on earth." (Psalm 58:10-11 LB) He was very motivated to see God vindicated; for people to see God in the proper light. If evil men were destroyed in such a way as to leave no doubt that it was divine judgment, not only would it encourage the godly to keep pressing on, but it would also reveal God's righteousness and equity to the rest of mankind.

Whatever the case may have been, Jesus Christ showed us a better way to win the lost. He was not only willing to see decent people saved, but just as willing to see the worst of sinners come into a saving relationship. He said, "love your enemies, do good to those who hate you, bless those who curse you, pray for those who mistreat you." (Luke 6:27-28) Paul added, "Do not be overcome by evil, but overcome evil with good." (Romans 12:21)

We can certainly utilize David's prayers regarding the destruction of demonic enemies, but when it comes to human beings, it is much better to lavish them with loving prayers.

AND HOW ABOUT YOU?

- *Are there people in your life who treat you as if you were their enemy?*
- *If so, have you matured in your faith to the point where you are able to ask God to extend His mercy to them? It is that sort of prayer that best reflects and glorifies the character of God.*

Unbelief and Silence

"I said to myself, I'm going to quit complaining! I'll keep quiet, especially when the ungodly are around me. But as I stood there silently the turmoil within me grew to the bursting point. The more I mused, the hotter the fires inside..." (Psalm 39:1-3 LB)

The Christian journey seems to take a relatively predictable course. It begins with the excitement of the new birth, when God is seen everywhere and in everything. It is the joy of the first love.

Over time, that excitement wanes and gives way to the maturing process. The growing believer settles into his new life with growing solidity. He experiences times of joy, times of sorrow, times of victory and occasional defeats. But through it all he is ever pressing on "toward the goal for the prize of the upward call of God in Christ Jesus." (Philippians 3:14) This is the normal course of events for a sincere believer who is maturing in his faith.

God is ever intent on deepening a person's faith. That process of deepening doesn't occur by pampering the believer with reassurance but by doing the very opposite. When the person matures to the place that he can handle such a trial, the Lord will purposely introduce circumstances that will actually make it difficult to believe in Him! In other words, He stretches a person's faith.

It seems that David was in such a trial when he penned Psalm 39. He was being plagued with the worst kind of doubts about the Lord. His mind was being overrun with accusing thoughts about God's goodness. Through the entire trial, he wisely restrained his words—especially around people who would only use such doubts to bolster their own skepticism.

I went through a period like this myself. It was awful! I had to be very careful about what I said in front of immature Christians for fear that I might discourage them. But I was in the spiritual battle of my life. I eventually came out the other end of that dark tunnel stronger in my belief in God's goodness than ever before. At the time I couldn't understand what was happening to me, but by the time I got through it, I came to see the good that God had accomplished within me through the experience.

Just be aware, dear one, that as you advance in the Christian journey, you will probably come to a point where you begin to doubt every conviction you have held. When that occurs, watch your words carefully around those of weaker faith, find a godly friend with whom you can vent your struggles and, most of all, take all your fears and doubts to the Lord. He is there with you, even if you can't sense His presence.

AND HOW ABOUT YOU?

- *Have you yet reached this point in your journey where it seems you are in a crisis of faith? If not, chances are you will before it is over. Just remember that God is holding your hand through that tunnel—even though He seems nowhere to be found.*

- *Are you prepared to be the godly friend someone else may need to help pray him through the dark period of his journey?*

Notes

Week Five: SATURDAY

God and Our Mistakes

> *"I sought the Lord, and He answered me, and*
> *delivered me from all my fears. This poor man cried and*
> *the Lord heard him, and saved him out of all his troubles...*
> *The angel of the Lord encamps around those who fear Him,*
> *and rescues them." (Psalm 34:4-7)*

The outpouring of gratitude expressed in this psalm came on the heels of an unlikely series of events in David's life. Saul had become jealous of the young captain who had led the king's armies to a number of tremendous victories over the Philistines. In his insane jealousy, Saul attempted to kill David, sending the young man fleeing for his life—right into Philistine territory.

Huh? Of all the places he could have gone, David went to Gath—the very hometown of Goliath, the Philistine champion he had slain. What was he *thinking*?

Perhaps he panicked and ran to the closest city outside Israel. Whatever the case may be, it was clearly a foolish decision—one which he made without the Lord's counsel.

But stupid mistakes are different from sinful actions. One can't help but think of the plight of Samson, who, some thirty years prior to this, also found himself in the hands of the Philistines. In his case, it was the lust for foreign flesh that drove him into Philistine territory. In the end, his eyes had been gouged out and he was thrown bleeding and whimpering into a foul prison cell.

ENTERING HIS COURTS

David's plight was not the result of sin, but of making a poor decision. As a result, he found himself alone in a hostile city, in the very grip of the enemy. One of the Philistines recognized him. "Is this not David the king of the land?" the man exclaimed. "Did they not sing of this one as they danced, saying, 'Saul has slain his thousands, and David his ten thousands'?" (1 Samuel 21:11)

David knew he was in deep trouble. Short of a miracle, he would not survive the day. He began crying out to God in his heart. The Lord came through by giving him the idea to act as though he had gone insane.

Before he knew it, he was safely out of the city, running back to the safer environs of Israel. He walked away from the frightening ordeal with the conviction that God had commissioned heavenly warriors to watch over his life.

Both Samson and David had been called by the Lord to accomplish a mission on behalf of His people. Their respective ordeals at the hands of the Philistines reflect the way the Lord worked on their behalf.

We may not face the wrath of Philistines, but we do have enemies bent on our destruction. We may make occasional mistakes, but if we will reject the soothing words of spiritual seducers, the Lord will always come to our aid—even in the case of stupid mistakes!

AND HOW ABOUT YOU?

- *Have you ever made a bad decision that put you in a difficult predicament?*
- *Did you cry out to God for His help? Didn't He come to your rescue just in time?*
- *God is not obligated to thwart the natural consequences of sin, but He can always be counted on to show compassion to His children when they make terrible mistakes.*

Week Five: SUNDAY

Blessed Forgiveness

"Blessed is he whose transgression is forgiven, whose sin is covered. Blessed is the man unto whom the Lord imputeth not iniquity..." (Psalm 32:1-2 KJV)

D avid opens this psalm by pronouncing a double blessing on those who have made peace with God regarding their sins. This psalm was almost certainly written after his great repentance regarding the Bathsheba affair as recorded in Psalm 51. One gets the sense that David wrote that psalm while in the throes of spiritual anguish; this psalm is more of a reflection after the fact.

The words expressed above are clearly an outburst of gratitude. After a long backslidden period of sin he is once again right with God. The Hebrew is actually more expressive than the King James translation renders it; his words were more like this: "Oh the blessedness…!"

The primary cause for this joy is that he has just emerged from a miserable period of spiritual darkness. He could have summed up his feelings in one simple statement (*i.e.,* "What a blessing to be forgiven of sin!"), but instead he used three different aspects of this disease of the soul to convey to the reader why it is such a blessing to receive a divine pardon.

The idea behind the word "transgression" (Heb. *pesha*) is very

113

closely tied to relationship. In this case, his sinful actions had brought about a rift between him and the Lord. And the longer he languished in his rebellious behavior, the further he drifted from God. By the time Nathan confronted him, David had seemingly brought himself right to the point of downright apostasy.

The word "sin" (Heb. *chătă'âh*) means to miss the mark, to fall short of the type of behavior delineated in the Law. The Bible clearly outlines how people are supposed to interact with God and how they are to interact with each other. Sin occurs when a person fails—in these interpersonal relationships—to live up to that standard.

The third term David uses is "iniquity" (Heb. *'âvôn*), which literally means to twist or distort something. Sinful actions may be forgotten by the person, but they leave a long lasting effect upon his heart. Sin contaminates every aspect of a person's inner life. His heart, emotions, will, thinking and even memory become corrupted by those spiritual crimes.

After having spent time considering the things he had done, the effects of his actions upon the Lord and others—and perhaps uppermost in his mind—the effects his sin had had on himself, in essence, David is bursting forth in praise saying, "Oh the blessedness of the man whose rebellious acts have been carried off and disposed of; whose selfish, abominable actions have been hidden from view; whose inward corruption has been cleansed!"

Having emerged from the long, dark tunnel of separation from God, David can clearly see the spiritual blessings which had been lavished upon him.

- *Have you ever gone through one of those seasons where you continue to live the outward Christian life, but your inward spiritual life feels dry as dirt? If so, I'm sure you learned that God always has a plan to draw us back to Himself. Praise the Lord that He never allows His sheep to stray too far away before He begins to call them back!*

- *Why not spend some time praising the Good Shepherd for His lavish blessings?*

WEEK
SIX

Week Six: MONDAY

Blessed Sincerity

"Blessed is the man... in whose spirit there is no guile."
(Psalm 32:2 KJV)

Yesterday we examined the great joy David experienced after having been forgiven of his transgressions in the Bathsheba affair. We briefly examined the three aspects of sin and the blessing involved with having both the record and the effects of those sins wiped clean.

But there was a fourth clause—offered above—which I purposely left out of yesterday's reading. I did so because David's thoughts take a slight turn and he now introduces what I believe is actually the key to repentance and forgiveness.

The word translated as "guile" (Heb. *remîyâh*) in today's verse has a fuller meaning than our English word seems to indicate. I believe that a better word to have used might have been "insincerity." "Blessed is the man... in whose spirit there is no insincerity."

We all know what a godly life David led in his earlier years, but once he began enjoying the luxuries of the palace life, it seems that his walk with the Lord grew stale. By the time he had his encounter with Bathsheba, a long period of spiritual lethargy had left him vulnerable to temptation. Each sin brought with it an ever greater deadness of soul. A year of languishing in this condition had left him hollow and miserable—ripe for a confrontation from a prophet. With life-and-death authority, he could have ordered the execution of the bold prophet on the spot. Instead, he responded by immediately humbling himself and entering a time of deep, heartfelt repentance.

The key to his response was the condition of his heart. Underneath all his folly and poor decision making was a sincere heart that compelled him to respond correctly. Had he been insincere he would have reacted much differently. He could have responded like so many do in such situations. He might have presumed upon the position of favor he had enjoyed with the Lord in the past: "God's grace covers all my sins!" Or he might have continued in the hypocrisy of acting as though he still enjoyed a right relationship with God.

No, during his prayer of repentance he said, "Sincerity and truth are what you require; fill my mind with your wisdom." (Psalm 51:6 GNB) Another psalmist would later sum up David's case: "The Lord is near to all who call upon Him, to all who call upon Him sincerely and in truth." (Psalm 145:18 Amp)

We all have those times when we get off-track spiritually, or even give over to blatant sin. But our loving Father will be sure to bring reproof and discipline at the perfect time. May we all respond as David did: with a sincere willingness to examine our hearts, acknowledge our sins and thoroughly repent.

And how about you?

- *Would you say that you have a sincere heart?*
- *How do you react when confronted with sin? Do you side-step the issue? Blame others? Attack the messenger? Or do you have a heart like David's that crumbles under the conviction of the Lord? The answer to these questions might serve as a good barometer of the sincerity of your heart.*

Week Six: TUESDAY

The Grand Plan

*"For the Lord declares, 'This is the King of my choice,
and I have enthroned him in Jerusalem, my holy city.'
His chosen one replies, 'I will reveal the everlasting
purposes of God, for the Lord has said to me, 'You are
my Son. This is your Coronation Day. Today I am
giving you your glory. Only ask and I will give you all
the nations of the world.'" (Psalm 2:6-8 LB)*

The conversation above, which occurred within the sacred precincts of the divine council in eternity past, is one of the most fascinating scenes found in Scripture. These four sentences outline the Grand Plan for mankind formulated "even before the world was made." (Ephesians 1:4 GNB)

God's declaration—His decree, His stated purpose—set into motion everything mankind has ever known or experienced. The material universe was created for the sole purpose of providing a stage, a backdrop, for the enacting of God's sovereign will for the human race. The formation of Israel, the Law and the Prophets, and, most of all, the advent of the Messiah were all part of the Plan.

The prophet Daniel was also taken back in spirit into eternity past and allowed to witness this divine interaction take place. He wrote, "I kept looking in the night visions, and behold, with the clouds of heaven One like a Son of Man was coming, and He came up to the Ancient of Days and was presented before Him. And to Him was given dominion, glory and a kingdom, that all the peoples, nations and men of every language might serve Him. His dominion is an everlasting dominion which will not pass away; and His kingdom is one which will not be destroyed." (Daniel 7:13-14)

When Jesus walked this earth, He certainly understood His part in God's strategy. He said, "All things have been handed over to Me by My Father..." (Matthew 11:27) "All authority has been given to Me in heaven and on earth." (Matthew 28:18) "The Father loves the Son and has given all things into His hand." (John 3:35)

According to the apostle Paul, "God did what he had purposed, and made known to us the secret plan he had already decided to complete by means of Christ. This plan, which God will complete when the time is right, is to bring all creation together, everything in heaven and on earth, with Christ as head." (Ephesians 1:9-10 GNB)

All of God's purposes have been challenged and opposed every step of the way by Satan and those who serve his interests. As we shall see tomorrow, the Lord's generous offer to mankind has largely been met with hostility and disdain. Though mankind rages against God's authority, seeks to stamp out every vestige of Christianity, and, at times, has even attempted to destroy every single copy of the Bible, the Lord reigns sovereign over the affairs of man.

God has a Grand Plan for mankind and He is calmly and systematically implementing it, in spite of people's opposition or lack of interest. Everything is unfolding exactly as He purposed from the very beginning.

What a reassuring word this is to us who will probably be alive to witness rebellious mankind's final insurrection against God and His Anointed at Armageddon. We need not fear because God has a Plan and, whether man or devil resists it, the Lord will accomplish His good purposes.!

AND HOW ABOUT YOU?

- *Are you living in harmony with God's plan?*

- *Are you living in subjection to Christ?*

- *Have you ever considered the bigger picture of God's involvement and oversight of man's history? Perhaps this would be a good time to reflect on how the Lord has been working out His great purposes down through the ages. It is a very comforting thought!*

Violent Opposition

"Why are the nations so violently moved, and why are the thoughts of the people so foolish? The kings of the earth have taken their place, and the rulers are fixed in their purpose, against the Lord..." (Psalm 2:1-2 BBE)

One would suppose that mankind would welcome the reign of a King such as Jesus Christ. What nation has ever been ruled by a more benevolent, just and trustworthy ruler than the Lord? But so thoroughly and pervasively has mankind been corrupted that the instant reaction to any suggestion of subjecting themselves to God's authority is met with universal rage.

It has been suggested that David penned this psalm just after he conquered Jerusalem, when the surrounding nations united together to attack Israel. Whatever the original intent might have been, the psalmist was (perhaps unknowingly) foretelling the crucifixion of Jesus Christ a thousand years later, and even more significantly, mankind's final insurrection against the establishment of Christ's kingdom on earth.

Why such violent resistance to this peaceful King? Because man does not want to be ruled by God. This is true both corporately and individually. People fiercely resist the gospel because they instinctively know that accepting God's authority over their lives means the end to self-will, pride, impurity and all of their other carnal passions. Adam Clarke describes the opposition as being "the unwillingness of rebellious nature to submit to the obligations of Divine laws, which cross the interests, and lay a restraint on the desires of men. Corrupt affections are the most inveterate enemies of Christ…"[1]

No single Bible version thoroughly captures the violent passion of the follow-up statement found in verse 3 so I will offer it in four different translations:

- Let us free ourselves from their rule, they say; let us throw off their control. (GNB)
- Let us break their chains, they cry, and free ourselves from slavery to God. (NLT)
- Let us tear off their chains and free ourselves from their restraints. (HCSB)
- Let us break their bands [*of restraint*] asunder and cast their cords [*of control*] from us. (AMP)

The sad fact of the matter is that the human race would prefer Satan's rule over their lives so long as they can continue to indulge their vices and have their way.

AND HOW ABOUT YOU?

- *Have you completely acquiesced to God's desire to extend His loving influence over every area of your heart and life?*
- *Or are there still pockets of resistance actively engaging in rebellion to His rule? The flesh rages when its dominion is threatened, but the Lord will conquer anyone's heart who is truly willing.*

God's Appointed Regent

> *"Jehovah said to my Lord the Messiah, "Rule as my*
> *regent—I will subdue your enemies and make them bow*
> *low before you." Jehovah has established your throne in*
> *Jerusalem to rule over your enemies. God stands beside*
> *you to protect you. He will strike down many kings*
> *in the day of his anger." (Psalm 110:1-2, 5)*

W e return once again to the sacred halls of the heavenly council chambers where, in eternity past, God the Father conversed with His dear Son regarding the future of mankind.

As we saw two days ago, the Lord has a "Grand Plan" He is unfolding for mankind. The last days are a time when God will bring all things under the subjection of the Messiah. As we saw yesterday, this will not happen without fierce resistance on the part of Satan and those who serve him.

Armageddon will be the climax of man's 6,000 years of rebellion. Satan will muster all his forces—every demon from hell and every impenitent sinner—to come against the Messiah and the new kingdom He will usher in. A thousand years after David was allowed this glimpse into the eternal councils of heaven, the apostle John was given a vision of this prophecy unfolding:

> "From His mouth comes a sharp sword, so that with it
> He may strike down the nations, and He will rule them with a

rod of iron; and He treads the wine press of the fierce wrath of God, the Almighty... And I saw the beast and the kings of the earth and their armies assembled to make war against Him who sat on the horse and against His army. And the beast was seized, and with him the false prophet who performed the signs in his presence, by which he deceived those who had received the mark of the beast and those who worshiped his image; these two were thrown alive into the lake of fire which burns with brimstone. And the rest were killed with the sword which came from the mouth of Him who sat on the horse, and all the birds were filled with their flesh." (Revelation 19:15-21)

What an amazing thing it is that, after thousands of years of God's purposes being unfolded for mankind, we will apparently live to see it culminate right before our eyes.

AND HOW ABOUT YOU?

- *Do you look forward to that day when God's perfect justice overtakes His enemies?*
- *Does the upheaval of earth life frighten you? You need not fear. If you belong to Christ, He will keep you through all the turmoil that will come upon this earth.*

God's Eternal Purpose

"The Lord frustrates the purposes of the nations; he keeps
them from carrying out their plans. But his plans endure
forever; his purposes last eternally." (Psalm 33:10-11 GNB)

During the past few days' studies, we have been considering God's Grand Plan for the redemption of fallen mankind. What a tremendous privilege and solemn responsibility to be able to consider such a theme. It is epic in its reach, timeless in its extension and irresistible in its motion. The Bible is the means by which the Lord has communicated this plan.

Not only did He outline the Plan fairly clearly in Scripture, but the Bible story (and subsequently, Church history) is the actual unfolding of that Plan. All that remains is the final consummation of His Plan upon earth and the inauguration of its eternal component.

And while God has His purposes for mankind on the whole, we must always remember that the whole is made up of individuals: people like you and me. Our lives make up a small part of that Grand Plan. This is a stupendous thought to consider. If we truly believed what Scripture tells us about this divine design for our lives, we would be tremendously fascinated with it.

There are two thoughts to consider regarding this subject. First, God's plan of redemption is available to be seen and understood by anyone who cares enough to look. The apostle Peter wrote that although the prophets of old wrote extensively on this subject, they didn't understand it. They were fascinated with the subject, in spite of the fact they were only allowed small glimpses of it. He also said this Plan was "so strange and wonderful that even the angels in heaven would give a great deal to know more about it." (1 Peter 1:12 LB)

When Albert Barnes considered the angels' fascination with this subject, he came to a startling conclusion:

> "How amazing, then, is the indifference of man to this great and glorious work... and that, busy and interested as he is in other things, often of a most trifling nature, he has no concern for that on which is suspended his own eternal happiness. If heaven was held in mute astonishment when the Son of God left the courts of glory to be poor, to be persecuted, to bleed, and to die, not less must be the astonishment than when, from those lofty heights, the angelic hosts look down upon a race unconcerned amidst wonders such as those of the incarnation and the atonement!"[2]

I suppose one of Satan's great sources of carnal delight is when he is able to distract Christians from such noble themes with the trifles of this temporal world. May it be one of the prayers of our hearts that God would renew our appreciation for, and interest in, the great Plan of redemption He has implemented for the saving of our souls!

And how about you?

- *Does your salvation still thrill your soul or has it lost its luster in your heart?*
- *Do you seem to be more taken up with God's kingdom coming to earth or to the cares of this temporal life?*
- *Why not ask the Lord to give you eyes to better see what He is doing.*

Notes

In The Beginning

*"Blessed is the man who walks not in the counsel of
the ungodly, nor stands in the path of sinners,nor sits in the
seat of the scornful." (Psalm 1:1 NKJV)*

The basic message of this opening psalm is simple enough: there are two distinct roads in life, each leading in opposite directions. There is a way of living which will take a person ever deeper into the lawless kingdom of darkness; it is a road which is characterized by emptiness, misery and futility, eventually leading to eternal doom. Likewise, there is another path which will lead a person into the ever-increasing riches of God's kingdom with all the peace and joy it offers.

The psalmist begins with a two-fold promise: if a person will avoid the ungodly persuasions of the world and instead subject his heart to the influences of the Word of God, he will enjoy a blessed life.

One would expect the book of Psalms to open with a rich description of life in God, but surprisingly, it opens with a negative statement. The clear inference is that a godly life is as characterized by what a person *doesn't do* as much as what he *actually does*.

In addition, the way the psalmist articulates this message is nothing short of brilliant. In one three-phrase statement, he not only offers an apt description of what makes up a godly person's life, but, at the same time, he paints a picture of a person entering into a life of sin.

At first glance, Psalm 1:1 seems to be written in classic Hebraic style: a spiritual truth is presented in multiple forms to reinforce its message.

But a closer look reveals that this is actually not the case. The three nouns the psalmist used reveal a sinful person's deepening digression into evil.

The "ungodly" represents the entire mass of humanity who live without God: *un*-godly. Matthew Henry poignantly describes them as people who "are unsettled, aim at no certain end and walk by no certain rule, but are at the command of every lust and at the beck of every temptation." This depicts mankind in their fallen condition.

The term "sinners" describes those who have not only ignored the Lord, but they have taken their rebellion a step further. They have given themselves over to the worship of sin. They are so taken up with their idolatry that their lives are defined by it. Thus, people are labeled alcoholics, sex addicts and so on.

The final descent into wickedness is when a person's heart becomes so darkened by evil that he makes himself a mouthpiece for the devil's mocking. What began as doubt, digressed into unbelief and finally settled into open cynicism. He has become so hardhearted that everything sacred is scorned with the utmost contempt.

This first verse serves believers with a loud warning to avoid all influences that originate within godless minds, because, once on that slippery path, it can eventually lead to destruction.

And how about you?

- *To what extent do you subject yourself to ungodly influences? For instance, how much time do you "sit" in front of a television, taking into your precious heart the perspectives and maxims of a godless world? Perhaps this first day of this study could provide you with an impetus to set clear-cut limits to what you watch and how much time you spend watching it. Just a thought.*

- *Are there other steps you could take to minimize your exposure to ungodly influences?*

Entering into the Blessings

*"Blessed is the man who walks not in the counsel of the
ungodly, nor stands in the path of sinners, nor sits in the
seat of the scornful." (Psalm 1:1 NKJV)*

Yesterday we examined the three basic groups of unsaved
mankind: unbelievers, sinners and mockers. Today we want to
look at a great two-fold truth offered by the psalmist: The human heart
is extremely impressionable, but we have been given the choice as to
what has access to it.

The "counsel of the ungodly" describes the prevailing maxims and
ruling principles of the unregenerate world. Unbelievers are seldom shy
when it comes to propagating their opinions about how people might
find happiness and fulfillment in life.

In the psalmist's day, a believer understood that he should avoid
the obvious hangouts of the drunks, criminals and prostitutes. This is
not so simple in the advanced culture in which we live, for Satan can
spiritually pollute us in the safety of our own homes through the various
forms of the media. For instance, on any given night, sitcoms and reality
shows offer the three people groups of Psalm 1:1 the opportunity to
fully vent their foul messages.

It should come as no surprise that Hollywood has been able to
rouse public sentiment against Christianity. What is astonishing to

me is the level of devotion Christians have to their TV watching. It seems that many are so addicted to entertainment—so unwilling to live without it—that it doesn't matter how wicked the content might be. Downright pornography is about the only form of programming that professing Christians are unwilling to tolerate.

I believe the key to Satan's success can be found in a biblical statement regarding a different subject. "Because the sentence against an evil deed is not executed quickly," wrote Solomon, "therefore the hearts of the sons of men among them are given fully to do evil." (Ecclesiastes 8:11) If I could slightly restate this verse I think you would get the sense about what I am saying: "Because people don't feel the effects of some forms of evil immediately, therefore they give themselves over to it completely."

It is true that the effects of television on the believer occur subtly and gradually. The television viewer doesn't lose his passion for the things of God, his yearning for God's presence, his rejection of the world's offerings, his shame of sinfulness, his abhorrence of evil right away. No, the change is subtle and gradual.

The message of the world always caters to the flesh and to self-love. Those who listen to that message inevitably take themselves out of God's blessing in life.

This first verse serves as a gateway to all of the blessings found throughout the entire book of Psalms. Let us heed the warning offered here and enter through God's prescribed entrance to all the joys He offers in this tremendous book.

- *Have you considered making a consecration unto the Lord about what you view? David wrote, "I will not have anything unworthy in my presence; dissolute behavior is odious to me; it shall not gain a hold on me." (Psalm 101:3 Har)*

- *If you've already made a commitment in this area, how well are you doing in keeping your commitment?*

- *Have you ever fasted from television? Are you willing to fast from it this week?*

WEEK
SEVEN

The Flourishing Tree

"But his delight is in the law of the Lord, and in His law
he meditates day and night. He will be like a tree firmly
planted by streams of water, which yields its fruit
in its season and its leaf does not wither; and in
whatever he does, he prospers." (Psalm 1:2-3)

We have been considering the opening verse of the book of Psalms and its negative benediction. The psalmist is now quick to add to it the other half of the blessing, for simply avoiding evil is not enough; we must also be spiritually fed.

The psalmist uses an analogy to illustrate his point. The man who derives pleasure from God's word is likened to a tree. This illustration conjures up three important truths.

First, the word "delight" (Heb. *chêphets*) means more than simply taking pleasure in something. It also involves the idea of a person's will: he chooses, or wills, to spend time in the Word. This spiritual maxim is reinforced in the fact that the tree has been purposely planted, as contrasted with one that grows in the wild. This man didn't just happen to become prosperous; he did so by the definite choices he made. He chose to plant himself where he knew his soul would prosper.

The second truth portrayed in this analogy is that this person will flourish regardless of outward circumstances. No raging storm will blow over this tree; no scorching heat of the Middle East will wither it. Every human faces difficult times, storms of life and adverse circumstances. If a person's roots have penetrated the depths of God, he will find that when those difficult times come, he will not shrivel up in the midst of it. In fact, while others around him are falling apart, his inner strength will stand out all the more clearly.

Lastly, spending quality time in Scripture assures the godly person that he will bear spiritual fruit in life. The Word of God has the efficacy to establish a godly perimeter in the mind of such a person: legislating his actions, correcting his errors, establishing Truth, and ultimately, directing the way he lives his life. The godly life that emerges from such study will always bear fruit for God. He has been impacted by studying the revelation of God's will and, in turn, will be sure to affect those around him.

If I were to rephrase this passage of Scripture, perhaps I would state it like this: "One of the great pleasures of the godly is to spend time soaking in the Word of God: something he does habitually and consistently. He can be compared to a tree whose roots have stretched forth deeply into a fresh stream; a tree which is full of life and bears luscious fruit for others even in the midst of a hot climate. Yes, this man has a rich and prosperous life in God."

And how about you?

- *Are you spending quality time in Scripture?*
- *Are you allowing the Holy Spirit to use His Word to search out your heart?*
- *Is the Word of God establishing a framework of thinking within you? Then surely you are a blessed person!*

Destiny of the Hypocrite

"But for sinners what a different story! They blow away like chaff before the wind. They are not safe on Judgment Day; they shall not stand among the godly... the paths of the godless lead to doom." (Psalm 1:4-6 LB)

After focusing on the life of the righteous in the first three verses of Psalm One, the psalmist takes a dramatic turn in the fourth verse when he shifts the focus onto the godless.

The reader is presented with a picture of an ancient farmer separating wheat berries from the unwanted husks. The chaff was light while the wheat berries had weighty substance. To separate one from the other, the farmer simply threw the whole mess up in the air and allowed the wind to carry the chaff away.

While this analogy offers an apt contrast of the godly and ungodly people found in the human race, it paints an even more vivid picture of the true and false believers who assemble together every Sunday in our churches. As Charles Spurgeon notes, "All our congregations upon earth are mixed. Every Church has one devil in it. The tares grow in the same furrows as the wheat. There is no floor which is as yet thoroughly purged from chaff. Sinners mix with saints, as dross mingles with gold."[1]

Hypocrites can become so adept at presenting a godly façade that sometimes only the Lord knows who are truly His. It is not so much the outward, observable life that differentiates the two, but the inward, hidden life.

The one outstanding characteristic about the religious pretender is that he feels perfectly at home in both the spiritual environment of the house of God and in the "counsel of the ungodly." He can move back and forth between both worlds effortlessly. He can sing hymns and listen to a sermon on Sunday morning and spend the rest of the day in the worldly atmosphere perpetuated through secular television. In fact, as long as there is nobody present with whom he must maintain his religious façade, he can watch the most carnal programming without the slightest concern.

Not only is the Lord watching what he does in secret, but He also sees what is truly going on inside him. Chaff is a fitting illustration of the inward life of the Christian imposter. Lacking the weighty character that is produced through true godliness, he attempts to make up for it by using words to cast an impression on people's minds of his piety. His act is as empty as the hot air he expels in the performance of it.

The message of Psalm 1 to the hypocrite could be narrowed down to one word in the second verse: delight. It would behoove each of us to sincerely ask ourselves what it is that offers us delight. Is it the godless entertainment of the world or the Word of God? That will give us a clear picture about where we stand with God.

AND HOW ABOUT YOU?

- *Where do you find your delight?*
- *If your pastor was able to secretly watch your actions throughout the day, do you think he would consider you to be a true believer?*
- *If you are living a godly life, one thing is certain: the Lord is building something weighty within you that will last the ages!*

Week Seven: WEDNESDAY

Bless the Lord!

*"I will bless the Lord at all times; His praise shall
continually be in my mouth." (Psalm 34:1)*

Written next to this verse on the worn page of my Bible is the
inscription: "6/11/95—8 guys walked out." At that point,
the Pure Life Ministries' residential program had been going for 5½ years
and was doing well. Nevertheless, some of the men began listening to
the complaints and criticisms of a rebellious student and packed up their
bags and left.

The morning after these men left, I opened my Bible and my eyes
fell on this verse. I knew the Lord was encouraging me in an unexpected
way. It was as if He were saying, "Steve, if you will focus on Me, your
heart will rejoice and your problems will diminish."

And that's exactly what I did. I began thanking God for all of
the many wonderful things He had done for me personally and for
the many men we had ministered to over the years. I was immediately
lifted out of my discouragement and was able to face the day with a
renewed hope.

Interestingly, five years before—almost to the day—the same thing
had occurred. The six-month-old program only had seven students
then—and six of them quit. It was devastating.

The difference was in how I handled this adversity. My "little
faith" sent me into a tailspin of despair and fear that I had completely

145

failed in ministry. I was much too aware of myself and not focused upon the Lord nearly enough.

What stands out to me all these years later is how much I had changed during those five years. I simply did not have the spiritual wherewithal in 1990 to bless the Lord in the midst of a painful experience. My first reaction to it was carnal and self-focused. But God was teaching me, to some extent, to live above the circumstances in which I found myself.

The Christian life is a journey of growth. Sincere believers will allow the Holy Spirit to work His wondrous change inside them. And isn't one of the primary purposes of a trial to test the person to see how he will react, to reveal the true level of maturity?

Immature Christians—such as the Steve Gallagher of 1990—may be able to open their mouths in praise when everything is going well, but they will not do so when facing adversity. More than likely their response will be one of complaining, fretting or even accusing the Lord.

Think back to the last trial you encountered and make an honest evaluation of where you are in your Christian journey. Allow this self-evaluation to encourage you on to a deeper trust in the Lord.

AND HOW ABOUT YOU?

- *Where do you see yourself in your spiritual journey? If you are fairly new to the Christian faith, you shouldn't demand a mature response of yourself to difficult trials. However, if you have been a believer for many years, you should be able to see a definite pattern of spiritual growth.*

- *Is there a specific affliction or trial your're dealing with right now? Perhaps you could write your own psalm of praise to the Lord despite this circumstance. Why not try? The Lord is good and His mercies endure forever!*

Notes

Notes

Open to Suggestion

*"The law of the Lord is perfect, restoring the soul;
the testimony of the Lord is sure, making wise
the simple." (Psalm 19:7)*

In the above verse we are presented with two distinct problems and a solution for each: a soul that must be restored and a "simple" person who needs wisdom.

Let's begin with the second phrase. The root for the word translated as "simple" is *pathah* which literally means "to open, or to be open." Scripture uses it figuratively to describe a person who is open to suggestion or easily seducible.

In my younger years, when I was utterly given over to sin, I possessed a devilish ability to discern girls who were needy for affection. I targeted girls who were vulnerable to exploitation. They were "open" to my advances because they wanted the attention I offered. The simple person David is referring to is someone who is similarly vulnerable to the wiles of the devil.

The first phrase of our verse seems to describe a simpleminded person who has been led astray by the enemy and has become ensnared in sin. In keeping with our illustration above, it is a girl who has given up her virginity and has subsequently gone from man to man until she has completely corrupted herself morally.

Eventually she begins to grasp the emptiness of sin and begins to look for a way out of its clutches. Under the influences of the Holy

Spirit she starts to see the extent her soul has been polluted. Is she beyond redemption? No!

Under divine inspiration, David promises that there is an invisible power inherent in Scripture that can transform her from the inside out. The law of the Lord—meaning the entire written revelation of God and His ways—is the spiritual mechanism available to heal the diseased soul. Moreover, it claims to be able to accomplish this monumental task perfectly, completely. Once it has established itself within a person's heart, God's Word has the power to build a sound mind and establish a love for holiness.

As this inner transformation is occurring, the Holy Spirit is busy utilizing the Word to accomplish yet another important task. The door of the heart—that has long stood open invitingly to the seducers of the spiritual realm—now has a guard stationed there to expose and block unwanted intruders who might attempt to gain entrance. A sign now hangs over that doorway: Closed. No Trespassing.

The truth is that all of us have allowed the enemy access to our souls. But as we spend meaningful time in the Word, we have its assurance that it has the power to protect us from the enemy's lies and to utterly change the direction of our thinking.

And how about you?

- *Can you see how the Lord has used His Word to close the door of your heart to "unwanted intruders?"*
- *Can you see how the Holy Spirit has used God's Word to restore your inner life from the ravages of past sin? What a blessing that God created us in such a way that He can always mend what has been broken!*

Our Times in God's Hands

"But as for me, I trust in You, O Lord, I say, 'You are my
God.' My times are in Your hand..." (Psalm 31:14-15a)

It isn't clear what was occurring in David's life when he penned these words, other than the fact that he was in real danger. The theme which stands out throughout this psalm is that his only hope of rescue is God—but he fully expects the Lord to protect him.

In the midst of his expressions of trust in the Lord, he makes what almost seems like a passing comment: "My times are in Your hand..." This word (Heb. *eth*) is sometimes translated as "seasons," and perhaps using that term would make this statement a little more illuminating for us: "My seasons are in Your hand..." All the various stages of my life: youth, adulthood and old age are all played out under Your watchful gaze. And all the different periods of my life: the times of prosperity and the times of adversity, the times of advance and the times of retreat, the times of activity and the times of waiting, they are all in Your hand.

David's son would later write: "There is an appointed time for everything. And there is a time for every event under heaven—A time to give birth and a time to die; a time to plant and a time to uproot what is planted. A time to kill and a time to heal; a time to tear down and a time to build up. A time to weep and a time to laugh; a time to mourn and a time to dance.... He has made everything appropriate in its time." (Ecclesiastes 3:1-11) Yes, and God oversees all of it in the life of the believer.

Entering His Courts

David understood that his entire life was under God's personal care, but he also understood that his days were numbered. His life would not end one day sooner or one day later than had been ordained by the Lord. He had entrusted his future into God's care. In fact, some translators narrowed the scope of David's statement to regard only his future:

- My fate lies in thy hands…(Mof)

- My future is in your hands. (NLT)

- You determine my destiny! (NET)

As one old time writer put it, "Till He give the command, nothing can force open the door of eternity for us; and when He does, nothing can keep us from entering it."

Whatever the case may be, it is clear that David saw a sovereign God's care over the entirety of his life. Let us lift our eyes off the temporal and catch a sight of the sovereign God who controls every stage of our lives—including its culmination.

And how about you?

- *Can you see how the Lord has watched over all of the different seasons of your life?*

- *Have you ever took time to really ponder how wonderfully He has covered you during those periods? Perhaps now would be a good opportunity to spend some time expressing your gratitude for His great care over your life!*

Week Seven: SATURDAY

Satan in the Psalms

> *"Oh my God deliver me from the hand of the*
> *lawless one, from the clutch of the perverse*
> *and ruthless one." (Psalm 71:4 Rhm)*

Let's be clear from the outset: when David discussed his enemies in the book of Psalms, he was referring to flesh-and-blood mortals. I can't think of a single instance that he purposefully spoke about demonic entities.

However, we must keep in mind that David's enemies were opposed to God's kingdom. In just the way that "spiritual forces of wickedness in the high places" do their utmost to overthrow the kingdom of God in our day, so too did the Philistines, Amalekites and even Saul's henchmen seek to destroy the divinely led government which David ruled.

We need to also keep in mind that those men were certainly influenced, incited and animated by devils. David surely understood—if only vaguely—that there was a spiritual adversary at work in the unseen realm around him. When he looked into the hate-filled eyes of a Philistine, he must have had some idea that the man was being driven by a spiritual force of wickedness.

Whatever the level of David's comprehension of the spiritual realm might have been, the fact remains that the same principles he expressed regarding those opposing God's kingdom can be carried over to the spiritual realm in which we find ourselves today.

Any believer who has been engaged in a true war for souls understands the reality of spiritual warfare. Surely such a person could join with David in lamenting, "Why must I suffer these attacks from my enemies?" (Psalm 42:9 LB) "Protect my life from the enemy's terrifying attacks." (Psalm 64:1 NET) And what veteran doesn't understand this cry: "I am troubled because of the voice of the cruel ones, because of the loud cry of the evil-doers; for they put a weight of evil on me, and they are cruel in their hate for me." (Psalm 55:3 BBE)

Yes, many of the prayers for divine vengeance found in the Imprecatory Psalms—as troubling as they may be for New Covenant believers—may certainly be used in our prayer times today. We face enemies every bit as real and ruthless as those which the psalmist faced.

"Satan in the Psalms?" Yes, he is mentioned throughout, if only by inference. Let us pray that he, his evil minions, his dark kingdom and all of his evil designs will soon be nullified and destroyed by the power of God.

AND HOW ABOUT YOU?

- *Can you sense the enemy's oppression in your life? That is actually a very good sign! Demons typically leave people alone so long as they are living carnal lifestyles, but when a believer begins to stand for righteousness—watch out! The enemy will surely attack.*

- *How adept are you at spiritual warfare?*

Human Utopia

*"Help us in this hour of crisis, the help that man
can give is worthless." (Psalm 60:11 JB)*

Who could ever forget the scenes of jubilant Germans tearing down the infamous Berlin Wall in November 1989? East Germans knew better than to accept the communists' claims that the wall was erected to keep capitalists out. Their country was little more than an enormous gulag.

The concept of socialism was the brain thrust of Karl Marx and Friedrich Engels, two nineteenth century atheists. The philosophy they set forth in their book, *The Communist Manifesto*, was their answer to the social injustices they saw at work under the capitalistic governments of their day.

They viewed capitalism as a system that fostered and encouraged man's inherent selfishness. They believed that it was capitalism that made man greedy and created an environment where the masses would be exploited for the good of the few. If the resources of the wealthy could be redistributed to the people, men would learn to live unselfishly. Only in such a setting as this could people be truly happy.

They set forth a plan that could only be inaugurated through revolution: the masses must rise up and overthrow their capitalistic governments. The assets of the country—banks, utilities, farms and corporations—must be confiscated by the new government and put into the hands of the people.

Such a scheme made sense to those who believed that the hope of mankind lies in man's ability to save himself. But, as David pointed out, such hopes are illusory.

It would be nearly seventy years before communists would have the opportunity to implement Marx and Engels' plan. It happened in 1917 when they overthrew the czarist regime in Russia and established a communist government in its place.

In spite of the fact that the Soviet Union had enormous resources at their disposal, communists were not able to construct the human utopia they had envisioned. From its earliest days communism was rife with problems, but it took seventy more years before their leaders would acknowledge to the world that socialism is not the answer to mankind's "crisis."

What Engels and Marx—and all those who later embraced their notions—failed to understand is that mankind's dilemma is not found in the imperfect environments produced by communism—or capitalism for that matter—but in man himself.

Man must be transformed from the inside out, and, humanistic psychology's claims notwithstanding, only God has the power necessary to accomplish such a change.

Christians instinctively understand that no secular government can provide the answer to man's longing for happiness. Yet, it's amazing how quick we are to think that a new home or a better job will bring us happiness. No, David's message is just as relevant to us as it is to socialists: Only God has the answers to man's unhappiness.

And how about you?

- *Where do you look for joy and fulfillment?*
- *Do you truly find it in the Lord or do you look for outside circumstances to provide it for you? God will bless you, truly bless you inside, as you turn to Him in sincerity!*

Notes

WEEK
EIGHT

Week Eight: MONDAY

Flagrant Sins

*"Moreover, keep me from committing flagrant sins; do not
allow such sins to control me. Then I will be blameless, and
innocent of blatant rebellion." (Psalm 19:13 NET)*

While it is true that all sins are equal in the sense that any of
them can damn a soul to hell, there is a wide range of evil
involved in different transgressions. These can range from a selfish motive
to crimes such as murder.

In our verse above, David is not referring to a particular sin; he is
alluding to the attitude that lies behind a person's sinful actions. Perhaps
a glance at some other Bible translations will help to bring clarity to
his statement. The NIV calls these transgressions "willful," the NASB
"presumptuous," the NLT "deliberate" and the NEB labels them "sins of
self-will." Whatever term is used, the overriding sense is that the person
has committed his act of sin in open defiance of God's authority; in His
face, as we would say.

Moses referred to this attitude when he said, "the person who does
anything defiantly... is blaspheming the Lord; and that person shall be
cut off from among his people." (Numbers 15:30)

In the verse before David's statement, he had asked the Lord to
acquit him of hidden faults. He follows this request with the plea found
in our passage: "Keep me from committing flagrant sins, do not allow
such sins to control me." While self-trusting souls tend to dismiss such
concerns, David knew full well that if he allowed sin to fester within him,

he could easily find himself falling headlong into one form of wickedness after another.

All sin begins in the heart. Contemplate any action long enough and it will only be a matter of time before one actually does it. Unfortunately, one sin begets another. It is the nature of sin to increasingly demand more indulgence. The more sin becomes entrenched in the heart, the more defiant the person becomes of God's authority. Before long, all pretense of spirituality is thrown off and the person becomes bold and reckless with his actions. The sinner becomes like the adulterous woman who "eats and wipes her mouth, and says, "I have done nothing wrong." (Proverbs 30:20)

How different was David's attitude! He had the wisdom to see where the steep slide into evil would take him. "By the fear of the Lord one keeps away from evil," his son would later write. (Proverbs 16:6) Yes, he feared the very sin that had the power to drag him away from God and eventually into hell itself.

The thought that he could actually become so given over to sin that he would do so with a brazen attitude was too much for him to handle.

And how about you?

- *Can you say that you have a tender heart like David's regarding sin?*

- *Do you hate every form of it in your heart?*

- *Do you fear the hold it can have on your life? If you can answer yes to these questions, then you are in a very blessed place in life because it means that you are continually turning to the Lord for His aid and deliverance.*

Week Eight: TUESDAY

Two Paths

*"Teach me Your way, O Lord; I will walk in Your truth;
unite my heart to fear Your name." (Psalm 86:11)*

I n his mind's eye, David could clearly see two paths perpetually
stretched out before him in life: the path of righteousness and
the path of rebellion.

On another occasion he prayed, "Make me know Your ways, O
Lord; Teach me Your paths." (Psalm 25:4) He earnestly desired to follow
the Lord in life. He wanted to know how the Lord saw things, how
He functioned, His perspectives and attitudes about people. He was
fascinated with everything about the things of God. Most of all, he
wanted to go wherever the Lord was leading.

By contrast, he was also aware of another way of life. "Concerning
the works of men, by the word of thy lips I have kept me from the
paths of the destroyer." (Psalm 17:4 KJV) He was utterly committed to
avoiding the ways of Satan. He had long since learned that "the way
of the wicked would perish." He saw that lifestyle as a long, drawn
out death; a tedious merry-go-round of sin and its consequences; of
temporal pleasures and their unsatisfying results.

Double-minded men don't see two paths stretching out before them
but three. These are people who do not want to give themselves over
to the paths of the destroyer, but neither are they prepared to throw
themselves completely into the direction of God's kingdom. They want

the best of both worlds. They want to keep their options open. They want to remain firmly in control over their own lives. What it boils down to is the desire to dabble in the indulgences Satan offers while on earth, but still spend eternity in the land of bliss.

While double-minded men tend to be unstable in life, the man who accomplishes much for the kingdom of God has a single-eyed focus in life. He isn't wavering "between two opinions." He has one great passion ruling his life: to live for God.

And how about you?

- *Can you include yourself in that small group who truly live their lives with fixed eye on the kingdom of God? Or do you find yourself drifting down paths you have no business being on?*

- *What would others—your spouse, your children, coworkers, etc.— say is the great ruling passion in your life?*

Week Eight: WEDNESDAY

A History Lesson

> *"Our forefathers have told us how you drove the*
> *heathen nations from this land and gave it all to us,*
> *spreading Israel from one end of the country to the other.*
> *They did not conquer by their own strength and skill,*
> *but by your mighty power and because you smiled*
> *upon them and favored them." (Psalm 44:2-3 LB)*

The psalmist is here referring to the occasion when Joshua and the people of Israel conquered the Promised Land. But it points out a greater truth as well: all of mankind's history has unfolded under the watchful eye of a sovereign God.

The truth is that history is made up of the individual timelines of billions of human beings interwoven during the past 6,000 years. Generations come and go, one being replaced by the next. Each one of us is part of the grand history of mankind. In my book, *The Time of Your Life in Light of Eternity,* I wrote the following:

> From His eternal vantage point, the Lord views the history
> of mankind in its entirety. He sees all the powerful rulers and
> great dynasties in an instant. The vast epochs of times gone
> by lay before Him…
>
> "'I am the Alpha and the Omega,' says the Lord God,
> 'who is and who was and who is to come, the Almighty.'"

165

(Revelation 1:8) In relation to man—the Lord is the beginning and ending and everything in between. This one sentence contains all that encompasses Time. He is the beginning of it; or, more accurately, He is the Creator of it. In the beginning, He initiated His grand program for mankind, and He will bring it to its conclusion. The very consummation of earth's ages will be wrapped up by the Lord Himself.

When one considers all that humankind's history has witnessed—the momentous events and all of the mundane acts of billions of souls, the great epochs of history and all of the fleeting moments of time, the great leaders and all of the common people, the Flood, the formation of Israel, the exile, the Birth and Death of Christ, the beginning of the Church, the Dark Ages, the closing scenes of Time—all of it has or will transpire under the ever watchful gaze of the Almighty.

Secular history books are written by those who only see part of the picture of mankind. Yes, they can recount world events, but what they can't see is that man is not the center of this story. The true center of mankind's history has been the sovereign King who has overseen it. These godless teachers are also clueless about the point of it all: individuals have been granted the opportunity to enter into a covenantal relationship with this great King which will secure them a place with Him throughout all eternity.

Yes, God's people conquered the pagan kingdoms that inhabited Canaan so long ago, but it was because the Lord was instituting His purposes through them and for them.

AND HOW ABOUT YOU?

- *Do you tend to see God looming largely behind the scenes of your life? Or does He seem small in your daily life?*
- *Perhaps this would be a good opportunity to commit yourself to a course of action that will give Him a larger place in your life. What steps could you take to make that happen?*

NOTES

Week Eight: THURSDAY

A Tight Spot

*"In my distress I cried out to the Lord. The Lord answered
me and put me in a wide open place." (Psalm 118:5 NET)*

About two months ago a loved one (I'll call her Brenda)
entered into a period of severe testing. She is a government
worker in a very liberal state. The trouble began when her new boss
showed up and found out that Brenda, who had been assigned to be
her chief assistant, was a Christian. She immediately began a campaign
of persecution toward her. For instance, she would pile upon her an
impossible amount of work and then publicly belittle her when she
didn't accomplish it all. In short, she did everything possible to pressure
Brenda into quitting her job.

Brenda informed Kathy and I about what was going on, pleading
in desperation for us to pray for her. And we did: every morning we
began interceding on her behalf before the throne of a very merciful
King. At first, our prayers were solely that she would be allowed to
transfer into a different department—a process she initiated almost
immediately. We love her and wanted to see her escape this unjust
treatment. But gradually, over the next two months, we found our
prayers changing: "Lord, grant her the grace and inner strength to
endure this trial. Accomplish Your good purposes in her life through it!"

There was no question that Brenda was in a "tight spot." In her
distress she was crying out to the Lord for relief. But God's ways are

not our ways. He answered her prayers, but did it in an unexpected way. Just this morning we received an email from her stating the following:

> By the way, your prayers are amazingly bringing the presence and sovereignty of the Lord so powerfully into my heart, mind and spirit. Although the culprit is still "attacking" – I'm experiencing such peace and joy in the face of it all, that I'm just astounded and actually wrestling with the thought of whether or not I really want to pursue the transfer.

Let's face it; trials are a major part of the Christian life. God is molding us into the image of Christ and preparing us for an eternity in heaven. It is only natural for us to cry out to God to rescue us from them, but what a tremendous testimony it is when we can truly come under those trials and endure them in the patience of God!

In Brenda's case, the Lord didn't take her out of it; He simply entered into that "tight spot" with her. By His very presence He made this tight spot a "wide open place;" a situation that suddenly became very bearable because He was in it with her.

And how about you?

- *When you encounter trials, is your first thought to escape them, or have you learned to submit yourself to God's will through it and ask Him to enlarge it with His wonderful presence?*
- *Can you recall any occasion when you opted to escape but now recognize it may have been more profitable to let God work things out differently?*

Meekness Under Hostility

"And all this has happened, Lord, despite our loyalty to you. We have not violated your covenant. Our hearts have not deserted you! We have not left your path by a single step." (Psalm 44:17-18 LB)

There is no consensus among commentators as to the occasion of the writing of Psalm 44. It is clear that it was penned at a time of great national hardship in spite of the fact that the Jewish people were faithfully serving God.

Throughout the 26 verses contained therein, the psalmist presented his case as to why the Lord should intervene in their current calamity. This could be summed up under four primary lines of reasoning: 1.) The Lord has helped the nation of Israel many times in the past, therefore they could expect Him to do so again; 2.) Israel's trust was not in their own ability to defeat their enemies but rested upon the Lord; 3.) the Jewish people had done nothing to deserve the harsh treatment they were currently facing; and 4.) that outsiders would come to see the merciful character of God if He would save His downtrodden people.

Consider what they were facing: their enemy was defeating and plundering them (vv. 9-10); they were being sold into slavery in the surrounding pagan nations (vv. 11-12); heathens were constantly ridiculing them and blaspheming their God (vv. 13-16); their country was being desolated to the point that "the shadow of death" was prevailing over it (v. 19); and finally, they were being given over to slaughter as if they were mere livestock (v.22).

The psalmist would have understood this treatment had his people been guilty of apostasy, but just the opposite was true. This was apparently occurring during a time when the nation was spiritually healthy. He could not wrap his mind around what seemed to him to be an incongruity. "Why won't You intervene, Lord?"

Yesterday we saw the same dynamic occurring in Brenda's situation, where she was hated for no other reason than that she was a believer. She too has asked God why He is allowing her to be treated so poorly.

And yet, Church history is replete with the stories of the persecution of God's people. The story of Betsy and Corrie Ten Boom is one such story. As they languished in Ravensbruck concentration camp, Corrie was astounded by the way her sister responded to the brutality of the guards there. While she struggled with bitterness and even rage at times, Betsy seemed only to have love for her captors. Corrie would eventually gain the victory in this battle, but their lives show the two ways believers will respond to persecution. One is to question God and turn angry toward one's antagonists; the other is to meekly accept God's sovereign dealings and to respond to hateful people with humility and love.

And how about you?

- *Do you know what it is like to respond with gentleness to unwarranted hostility? Or do you move right into a retaliatory spirit when you feel you are being treated unfairly?*

- *How well prepared are you to handle the increase in persecution Jesus said would accompany these Last Days?*

Week Eight: SATURDAY

Prideful Reasonings

"The wicked man hath said in his heart, I shall not be moved: for I shall never be in adversity." (Psalm 10:6 KJV)

D avid uses the phrase, "hath said in his heart," three times in Psalm 10 to describe the thoughts of a proud and wicked man. In this verse the godless man imagined his prosperity continuing forever while in verses 11 and 13 he expressed his belief that God would not hold him accountable for his actions.

Such foolish musings are to be expected of a rebel who has determined to live a wicked life. However, this line of thinking isn't confined to evil men. For instance, when the Lord promised Abraham that Sarah would be impregnated, "Then Abraham... said in his heart, 'Shall a child be born unto him that is an hundred years old? and shall Sarah, that is ninety years old, bear?'" (Genesis 17:17 KJV) Thus, the father of our faith temporarily gave over to blatant unbelief.

Likewise, we later find David himself entertaining questionable thoughts within his heart. After being on the run from Saul for some time, he decided to consult himself rather than the Lord. "David said in his heart, I shall now perish one day by the hand of Saul: there is nothing better for me than that I should speedily escape into the land of the Philistines..." (1 Samuel 27:1 KJV) He then moved his entire army into the territory of the Lord's enemies.

And finally, just after God graciously committed the northern tribes of Israel into his care, "Jeroboam said in his heart... If this people go up to do sacrifice in the house of the Lord at Jerusalem, then shall the heart of this people turn again unto... Rehoboam king of Judah." (1 Kings 12:26-27 KJV) His musings brought him to the conclusion that he should set up idolatrous altars in Israel as an alternative to the Temple in Jerusalem.

The truth is that every story in the Bible is an example of someone behaving in some manner—whether good or bad—after first pondering his course of action within his heart. Nevertheless, examining the various usages of this phrase regarding the human heart provides a nice cross-section of humanity—from two of the godliest lives found in the Bible all the way down to the wicked atheist.

Each of these examples holds one thing in common: when the person consulted his own heart rather than the Lord for direction in life the results were disastrous. May this little exercise serve as an apt reminder for all of us to always, always consult God before making important decisions.

And how about you?

- *Do you make important decisions by your own reasonings or do you truly wait on God for His direction?*
- *Why not write a prayer of commitment to the Lord that you purpose to wait on His direction for the important decisions you must make in life. Now would also be a great time to lay before Him any specific decision you are wrestling with today.*

The Great Day

> *"Seventy years are given to us! Some even live*
> *to eighty. But even the best years are filled with pain*
> *and trouble; soon they disappear, and we fly away...*
> *Teach us to realize the brevity of life, so that we may*
> *grow in wisdom." (Psalm 90:10, 12 NLT)*

The first lie that mankind was confronted with was when the serpent told Eve, "You surely will not die!" (Genesis 3:4) Now, we all know that the primary point this foul snake was making to this hapless woman was that she could step out in self-will without fear of consequences. God had told her and her husband that if they ever ate of the tree of life that they would die. The devil came along to refute that. And one of the most deceptive aspects of sin is that it doesn't usually bring about instantaneous physical death. Instead, it brings about a slow-acting spiritual death.

But I believe the devil's words ("You surely will not die!") reflect another lie: the notion that death is a long way off. Indeed, the devil does everything within his power to keep people focused upon the moment, to the neglect of the eternal. Of course, an addiction is the perfect example of someone who goes through life living for momentary pleasure, in spite of the fact that it will ruin his life and eventually send him to hell.

Most live without the slightest concern about their final day on earth. They think about today, this day—the now. But humans have no guarantees about tomorrow.

Entering His Courts

I reflected on this reckless tendency one time as I watched a BBC documentary on World War II. I can still remember the faces of those young German soldiers who were marching in a victory parade in Berlin, flush with tremendous victories over Holland, Belgium and France. Those were heady days! Their songs rang through the night everywhere they went. Yet, a couple of videos later (within months of that victory parade), 300,000 of these same soldiers lay frozen to death in a cruel Russian winter.

Yes, the enemy had successfully obscured the fact that they could meet death at any time. Their final day on earth, and the moment of judgment that would instantly follow it, seemed a long way off. They were happy to live for the moment, ignoring the eternal.

And how about you?

- *Do you live your life as if it will go on forever, or do the decisions of your daily life reflect the wisdom of someone who understands the brevity of earth life?*

- *Is there a situation you need to rectify, or perhaps a relationship you need to reconcile, before it's too late?*

~Notes~

WEEK

NINE

Sorrowful Sowing

*"Those who sow in tears shall reap with songs of joy.
A man may go out weeping, carrying his bag of seed;
but he will come back with songs of joy, carrying
home his sheaves." (Psalm 126:5-6 NEB)*

There is an undeniable aspect of Christianity that involves sorrow. Indeed, the central figure of the Christian faith is "the man of sorrows." (Isaiah 53:3) He is also the One who said, "Blessed are you who weep now, for you shall laugh… Woe to you who laugh now, for you shall mourn and weep." (Luke 6:21, 25)

Jesus brings out a very important element to this spiritual dynamic with the words "now" and "shall." "Now" clearly refers to the "here and now" of earth life. In keeping with His normal way of speaking, Jesus offers only a fearful black-and-white contrast.

On the one hand, there are those whose primary focus during their time on earth is the temporal enjoyment that appeals to one's lower nature. They are forever searching out new forms of entertainment and sources of pleasure that will distract them from their spiritual responsibilities. Yes, there is laughter, but it is the superficial type—the kind of mirth that wells up from an empty heart and can offer no more than a momentary reprieve. Such superficial activities are ever pushing them down a road toward that horrible world of woe.

But Jesus also pronounces a blessing—an invocation of eternal prosperity—on those who are forced to endure hardship for His sake during their stay on earth. One day they will enter that wonderful world of joy where one's inner exuberance will be constantly bubbling up in the kind of jubilant laughter that comes from a full heart.

There is no question that the Christian life is full of various kinds of sorrow. Godly evangelists weep over lost souls. Godly pastors grieve over people they have poured their lives into who respond with hatred. Godly missionaries quietly suffer when the people they are called to minister to use them for self-serving purposes. Godly deans of Bible schools live with the distress of seeing students they love making one bad decision after another. Godly wives mourn over wayward husbands, while godly parents long to see their prodigals return home. This is all part of the price of truly caring about the eternal plight of other people.

Yet, every type of suffering we are called to endure on earth will be enormously repaid in glory. The very scars we carry from our sufferings will become our crowns in heaven. In the same way that soldiers are honored for their deeds of heroism on the battlefield, so too will earnest believers be honored for what they suffered for Christ's sake during their time on earth. Yes, now is often a time of weeping, but then shall be a time of laughter!

AND HOW ABOUT YOU?

- *Are you living for the enjoyment of the day, or are you bearing the burden of hurting souls?*
- *Specifically when it comes to life's sorrows, do you live with a temporal or an eternal mindset?*

Two Shepherds

"Death herds them like sheep straight to hell..." (Psalm 49:14 MSG)
"Because the Lord is my shepherd, I have everything I need!"
(Psalm 23:1 LB)

In the spiritual realm, there are two shepherds: Jesus Christ and Satan, the angel of death. Man's time on earth is a probationary period meant to reveal which shepherd people will choose to follow. Consider the differences found in these two shepherds, their flocks and the eventual destinations of each group.

Jesus Christ truly is "the good shepherd [who] lays down His life for the sheep." (John 10:11) He has proven His willingness to go after the lost sheep—even the one sheep whose willfulness has led him astray to the point of finding himself lost. Jesus will go to battle with any wolf or lion to save one of His sheep—even to the point of laying down His own life. Depending completely on what His sheep need, He leads them beside "green pastures," "quiet waters," or even through the "valley of the shadow of death." Every new experience is meant for the eternal good of His beloved.

Satan, on the other hand, is rightly known as the Destroyer; he is the personification of Death itself. He is utterly selfish—everything he does is ultimately done to satisfy his own lust for blood. He doesn't lead people. At first, he uses the oily words of a temptress to lure them ever deeper into sin. He keeps them on the road to perdition by constantly inflaming their lust for sin—but it is an itch that can never be satisfied.

Rather than feeling an increasing sense of fulfillment in their pursuits, they become increasingly more agitated and miserable.

Who are the sheep of Satan's pasture? According to Psalm 49, they are those whose hearts are completely fixed on earth life. "Their inner thought is that their houses are forever…" (Psalm 49:11) They are happy to indulge themselves in Satan's allurements because they live for temporal pleasure. If they show an interest in spiritual things it is only superficial and hypocritical.

The flock which Jesus leads is of a different sort. They know their Master's voice and follow Him wherever He leads. Why? Because they have come to understand that He is goodness personified; that He is trustworthy; that He only has their best interests in mind. It is this willingness to be led—to obey—that characterizes them as part of the flock of Jesus Christ. One day He will lead them straight into eternal life.

And where is Satan's flock headed? The unbeliever will one day discover to his horror that he has been terribly deceived. "He is torn from the security of his tent, and they march him before the king of terrors." (Job 18:14) He consigned himself to Satan's kingdom on earth and will remain with him forevermore.

AND HOW ABOUT YOU?

- *Would you say your life is one that is led to the quiet waters of God's kingdom, or does it seem more like one that is being driven by a lust for the things of this world?*
- *It is one thing to call Jesus, "Good Shepherd," but quite another to follow Him. Which shepherd is your heart following?*

~Notes~

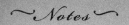
Notes

Judgment of God's People

*"Our God is coming, but not in silence; a raging fire is in
front of him, a furious storm around him. He calls heaven
and earth as witnesses to see him judge his people. He says,
'Gather my faithful people to me, those who made
a covenant with me...'" (Psalm 50:3-5 GNB)*

This is a fascinating scene presented long before the greater
revelations of Judgment that would be given to First Century
believers. Although it wasn't very clear to the psalmist, the Judge being
referred to here would be the Messiah of Israel. Jesus said as much in
John 5. (cf. John 5:22-29; also Matthew 25:31-32). This fact was later endorsed
both by Peter (Acts 10:42) and Paul (Acts 17:31).

However, this particular judgment scene doesn't seem to encompass
all of mankind, but is apparently a judicial proceeding confined to
those who had claimed to enjoy the benefits of being in covenant with
God. This probably refers to Old and New Testament "believers;" but
whatever the case may be, it is clear that the reality of their claimed
relationship with God would be evidenced by the way they lived their
lives. The Lord is quoted again later in this psalm: "But to the wicked
God says, 'What right have you to tell of My statutes and to take My
covenant in your mouth? For you hate discipline, and you cast My
words behind you.'" (Psalm 50:16-17)

Clearly there were those who claimed to be God's people who

had proven to be unfaithful. Charles Spurgeon held out no false hope for such unfaithful people. Of these two verses he writes the following:

> "Do you dare to teach my law to others, and profane it yourselves? What impudence, what blasphemy is this! …You talk of being in covenant with me, and yet trample my holiness beneath your feet as swine trample upon pearls…
>
> In these last days there are pickers and choosers of God's words who cannot endure the practical part of Scripture; they are disgusted at duty, they abhor responsibility, they disembowel texts of their plain meanings, they wrest the Scriptures to their own destruction. It is an ill sign when a man dares not look a Scripture in the face, and an evidence of brazen impudence when he tries to make it mean something less condemnatory of his sins, and endeavors to prove it to be less sweeping in its demands. How powerful is the argument that such men have no right to take the covenant of God into their mouths, seeing that its spirit does not regulate their lives!"[1]

AND HOW ABOUT YOU?

- *I realize that you must believe yourself to be a child of God, but does your life actually bear that out? For instance, do you love or hate God's discipline?*
- *One day we will all stand before Christ. The way we have lived our lives won't save us but it will evidence whether or not we had truly partaken of the new covenant. If you are in doubt about it, just begin to earnestly ask God to make it clear to you one way or another. Let Him and Him alone grant you the assurance of faith.*

GPS

*"I wander about like a lost sheep; so come and look for
me, your servant, because I have not neglected your laws."
(Psalm 119:176 GNB)
"For the Lord watches over all the plans and paths of
godly men..." (Psalm 1:6 LB)*

Kathy and I were in town visiting our friends Phil and Beth. I was driving the four of us to a restaurant and put the address into our GPS system. Beth is a very sweet woman, if a little naïve, and had never seen a GPS system before. As we were driving to our location, a lady's voice would announce each turn we needed to make as we approached the street. Beth was clearly impressed by this. On an impulse I kiddingly fabricated a completely farfetched scenario to explain it. "There's a lady sitting at her computer in Des Moines who is tracking our car on her screen. She just tells me where I need to turn." This astounded Beth and it wasn't until the rest of us burst out laughing that she figured out that I was just putting her on.

But isn't it wonderful to know that our lives are constantly on "God's screen?" He is ever watching His loved ones as they continue on their respected journeys of life. "For the eyes of the Lord are intently watching all who live good lives, and he gives attention when they cry to him." (Psalm 34:15 LB) What a wonderful assurance this is as we make our way through the "dangers, toils and snares" of life!

ENTERING HIS COURTS

As believers, we have been called to the Narrow Path. It is the Word of God that directs our paths. By spending time in Scripture every day, we are receiving a constant influx of God's mind on how to live our lives. Let's face it; just like dumb sheep that are "prone to wander," we humans have a built-in default system of our own which is continually attempting to lead us astray. We desperately need God's law to be entrenched in our hearts so we will have the sense not to go off track. Those who do not have an established time in the Bible every day are extremely susceptible to being deceived.

However, so deeply embedded in our natures is this tendency to go astray, that even those who are regularly being fed by Scripture still have their times of wandering off the "straight and narrow." In fact, there are times when God's children wander so far off track that they don't realize what they have done until they are completely lost and bewildered.

But the Lord is incredibly patient with us and, just like a good GPS system, He simply recalculates our position and gives us new directions to get back on track.

AND HOW ABOUT YOU?

- *Do you have a time set apart to meditate upon Scripture every day?*

- *Do you sense His continual care over your life?*

- *Do you look to Him for guidance about decisions? Or are you just doing life on your own, loosely following the "rules" of evangelical Christianity?*

Rage and Peace

"Why do the heathen rage... against the LORD... saying,
Let us break their bands asunder, and cast away
their cords from us." (Psalm 2:1-3 KJV)

"The LORD is my shepherd, I shall not want. He makes me
lie down in green pastures; He leads me beside
quiet waters." (Psalm 23:1-2)

The two short passages provided above offer drastically different pictures that are worth considering.

Psalm 2 is a prophecy about mankind's final hours upon earth. The picture we are presented is a worldwide tumult. What explanation can there be for the world's entire population to be in a rage? I believe I know the answer.

We live in a world of tremendous technological advance. This has allowed most people of this world to taste various pleasures and forms of entertainment that have left them longing for more. Lust of any kind is a hellish existence which causes people to live in a state of continual dissatisfaction. In fact, the more a person gives over to his lust, the more driven he will be to satisfy it. A sweating, shaking heroin addict is a vivid picture of what happens in a lustful person's soul.

The Bible seems to indicate that the years leading up to the Great Tribulation will be a period of intensifying lust. Then God will begin to let loose terrible plagues and catastrophes. Revelation 18 is a depiction of the world and all of its allurements collapsing as men cry out in anguish at their loss.

Those who are ever grasping for the devil's token pleasures will ultimately—whether at the end of this age or in hell itself—live in a constant state of frustration and agitation that the Psalmist rightly calls "rage."

Consider the contrast to this spirit offered in the opening verses of Psalm 23. Those who allow the Lord to lead them—rather than the inherent lusts of the flesh—will find a life of contentment and fulfillment. What a tranquil and serene picture is offered in the words, "I shall not want." Not only will the true believer not lack anything necessary for his life, but he will also be marked by his inner tranquility. He will not be driven by "want"; the lust or the obsession with the fleeting pleasures of this world.

In a culture that caters to every whim a person might want to satisfy, how can believers live a calm, contented life? The allegory of Psalm 23 provides the two primary answers.

First, the Good Shepherd will never lead His people into a lust-filled life. If they are truly His sheep, they will know His voice and will be led by His staff. He will keep them in perfect peace. They will not be wild goats, running all over the countryside in a vain and futile endeavor to find grass that always seems greener elsewhere.

Second, they will be known for the regular intervals they spend "beside quiet waters." It is the very thing you are doing right now, dear one. You have quieted your soul and are spending precious time in His presence. It is there that your spirit will be refreshed and your flesh will be subdued.

Let us continue on our journey with a clear sense about the different destinations which lust and contentment will take us.

AND HOW ABOUT YOU?

- *When you examine the way you live your daily life, would you consider yourself to be a person of calm contentedness, or one who is driven by desire for greener grass elsewhere?*
- *Do you recognize, and make arrangements for, those times of refreshing "beside the still waters" when you need them?*

Who's Building the House?

> *"If Yahweh does not build the house, in vain the masons*
> *toil; if Yahweh does not guard the city, in vain the*
> *sentries watch." (Psalm 127:1 JB)*

However applicable this profound verse might be to construction projects and sentry duty, the deeper truth refers to the spiritual work done through us. Both clauses in this verse are making the same point: attempting to do anything in God's kingdom in the flesh is an utter waste of time.

It also implies another truth: there must be a proper balance in human effort and faith-filled trust in the Lord. Many times I have witnessed ministers (including myself) err in one direction or the other.

Some imagine that they are going to "trust God" to accomplish important kingdom work when the reality is that they simply don't want to pay the required price involved in true gospel work. They piously say they are waiting on the Lord, but in truth, they simply want everything handed to them. Such was the servant who "hid his talent in the ground" and has had the epitaph written on his life that he was a "wicked, lazy slave." To live out the love of God to needy people is no easy task. It means bearing them to God in prayer, sharing in their sufferings, sometimes even being the object of their hostility. The apostle Paul was a shining example of someone who bore the marks on his body of someone willing to pay a dear price to bring the gospel to the lost.

On the other extreme are those who attempt to do God's work in their own strength. I would break this group into two categories. First, there are hirelings who are in it for their own purposes. If they have a prayer life at all it is very minimal and self-focused. They are driven by ambition and measure results in terms of outward signs of success. They are building a house, but it is like the monument Saul built for himself. When they stand before God one day—and stand they will—they will be confronted with the reality that all of their efforts in God's name have really been for themselves.

The second group of people who fall into the category of depending upon their own efforts are those who have sincerely attempted to serve God but for one reason or another, have gradually and unknowingly slid into self-trust. In our hectic day and age, it is very easy for ministers to become so busy that a subtle change begins to take hold of their efforts. When overwork begins to drain them spiritually, they can get out of the flow of God's grace. Before they realize what has happened, they are operating in the flesh, worrying about the lack of results, doubling their efforts, becoming even more taxed... well, I think you can see how a person can slide into self-efforts without realizing it. This is a struggle I understand all too well.

AND HOW ABOUT YOU?

- *I know that God has called you to work in His vineyard in some capacity; do your efforts reflect someone who is passionate about furthering God's kingdom or do you just "trust God" to do everything?*
- *Or perhaps you are one who is busy with the Lord's work but depending more upon your own efforts than God's provision. Take it to the Lord in prayer and ask Him to purify your motives and deepen your faith in Him.*

Week Nine: SUNDAY

My Heroes

*"The godly people in the land are my true heroes! I take
pleasure in them!" (Psalm 16:3 NLT)*

A friend of mine has been a missionary to Sudan for the past
fifteen years. It is unquestionably one of the most hazardous
places on earth for an American minister to labor. And when he comes
home on furlough, his denomination showcases him as a modern-day
hero of the faith for all to emulate and admire.

And who among us hasn't been thrilled by the stories of saints like
Brother Andrew, who smuggled Bibles into communist countries in the
'60s; or David Wilkerson, ministering at the same time to the dangerous
gang members of New York City? These are people who risked their lives
for the sake of bringing the gospel to people in need.

Yet there is another kind of Christian hero that goes largely unnoticed
on earth. I am referring to simple Christians who bravely invite God to
transform them into the likeness of His Son, Jesus Christ.

Like David did so many centuries ago, their cry to the Lord is, "Search
me, O God, and know my heart; try me, and know my anxieties; and see
if *there is any* wicked way in me, and lead me in the way everlasting." (Psalm
139:23-24) It is a most frightful prayer and should never be offered lightly.

Such a petition opens the door for the Holy Spirit to do a thorough
investigation of one's entire inner being: to expose and root out every
noxious attitude, every prideful inclination and every selfish motive. And,

197

of course, the unspoken "rider" to this petition is the understanding that the Lord will institute circumstances into the person's life that will begin to purge this poison out of him.

This is no small thing for it is, in essence, the signing over of one's rights to Another. In our legal system, every American possesses certain "inalienable rights" as a U.S. citizen. One individual may sign over decision-making rights to another, but this is only done in extreme circumstances (e.g. an incapacitated elderly person).

The truth is that when a person enters into a covenant relationship with God, he forfeits all rights of self-determination. In our current Church culture, it has become popular to proclaim all of the benefits of this relationship, but what are seldom discussed are the responsibilities that are inherent in it.

It is God's prerogative to deal with His people as He sees fit and yet, true to His humble nature, He mostly allows believers to choose for themselves their level of intimacy with Him. Very few actually allow God the kind of carte blanche access to their hearts that will make for a deep relationship.

Those who do are rarely afforded on earth the degree of honor awaiting them in heaven. And their stories don't typically offer the sort of thrilling exploits that are the stuff of biographies. Yet, in God's economy, their courage is every bit as important. Such saints have a story that would thrill the holiest of angels because they have faced the most frightening thing one can encounter on earth: the truth about themselves.

While others are at ease in this world and satisfied with their current spiritual condition, these sincere saints are struggling through the great issues of the faith, fighting to lay hold of God in a meaningful way. They well understand what the psalmist meant when he said, "Weeping may last for the night, but a shout of joy *comes* in the morning." (Psalm 30:5) Theirs is a life of much struggle, but through it all, God is having His way in their hearts and in their lives.

Such people may not be paraded around by the great denominations of the day, but God will use them nonetheless—and it will all be to His glory!

AND HOW ABOUT YOU?

- *Do you lead a life that would be considered heroic in the halls of heaven?*
- *Do you allow God to have His way within you?*
- *Do you sincerely ask Him to purge the poison of the self-life out of you?*

WEEK

TEN

WEEK
TEN

When God Withdraws

"Will the Lord abandon me forever? Will He never again
display kindness? Has His merciful love completely
disappeared?" (Psalm 77:7-8a Har)

One of the common themes expressed by the various psalmists is that they had experienced seasons when the Lord seemed to pull away from them. Of course, David felt this after being rebuked for his affair with Bathsheba. "Banish me not from thy presence," he cried; "deprive me not of thy sacred Spirit." (Psalm 51:11 Mof) What could be more horrible for a believer than the sense that God had expelled him from His presence?

But there is a different sort of banishment that the Almighty occasionally metes out to His loved ones. And it doesn't seem to be connected to carnality, worldliness or blatant sin.

I'm not referring to carnal Christians who haven't experienced true intimacy with God. It only makes sense that they would not know what it's like to enter the inner precincts of the Lord's throne room. I'm also not referring to the dry spells that every believer occasionally encounters. And I'm definitely not talking about the separation from God a person feels because of outward sin.

What I am referring to is the very real sense that God is no longer there—in spite of the fact that the person hasn't done anything "wrong."

I used to read statements like these made by Asaph and assumed I knew all about it. After all, there had been many times that the Lord seemed distant from me. But it wasn't until the Lord took me through very deep waters that I realized how superficially I had understood the psalmist's cry.

I am convinced that every true believer will eventually go through a period when—through no fault of his own—God withdraws His presence. The sons of Korah experienced this as well. They went through a time when the Lord seemed to turn away from them and give them over to the hands of their enemies. They wrote, "And all this has happened, Lord, despite our loyalty to you. We have not violated your covenant. Our hearts have not deserted you! We have not left your path by a single step. If we had, we could understand your punishing us in the barren wilderness and sending us into darkness and death." (Psalm 44:17-19 LB)

What I learned during my trial was that—even though I had not indulged in worldly living or known sin—my passion for the things of God had become stagnant. I had allowed myself to get into certain spiritual ruts. Un-Christlike attitudes had formed within me that were not going to be uprooted without a certain degree of drastic chastisement.

One day while I was in the middle of this period, the Lord spoke to me and said, "I am breaking up the fallow ground." It took some time before I came to understand what He was saying to me. He was allowing me to feel spiritual deadness because He wanted to give me a fresh beginning. And He did it! Losing the sense of God's felt presence was extremely distressing to me, but now I am so thankful for what He did for me through it.

AND HOW ABOUT YOU?

- *Have you ever experienced the sense that God had withdrawn from you? If not, rest assured it will probably come your way and when it does, rest in the fact that the Lord loves you and is disciplining you for the purpose of deepening your faith and sweeping away unwanted ruts.*

- *Are you thoroughly convinced that the Lord disciplines those whom He loves?*

- *What can you do to help someone else through their season of losing the sense of God's presence? What would you want others to do for you?*

Week Ten: TUESDAY

Mercy Ruts

*"Remember, O Lord, Thy compassion and Thy
lovingkindnesses, for they have been from of old. All the
paths of the Lord are lovingkindness and truth to those
who keep His covenant and His testimonies."*
(Psalm 25:6, 10)

Yesterday I mentioned that I had allowed myself to get into certain spiritual ruts. What Christian doesn't know the misery of being stuck in a rut? Life seems tedious, predictable, and even miserable. One tedious day gives way to another. The term "rut" typically describes habitual behavior that is unhealthy or even destructive. A person has lived a certain way for so long that it seems that he is destined to continue in this lifestyle for the rest of his life.

In the natural world, a rut occurs in a dirt road when vehicles continue to drive over it in the same location. People tend to drive in the same part of the road as others, and over time their tires begin to develop a groove in the road. The deeper the groove, the more others tend to fall into it.

The word "rut" has developed a negative connotation, but it can also be used in a positive sense. "All the paths of the Lord are lovingkindness and truth…" The Lord has been operating under these guiding principles (if I could call them that) "from of old." They have become so established in His typical way of dealing with His people that they could certainly describe a major aspect of His lifestyle.

Consider your own past dealings with the Lord. Can't you look back on your life and see one instance of His mercy after another? Hasn't He always been utterly truthful with you—even though at times that truth hurt? Wouldn't you say that He has abundantly proven to you that lovingkindness and truth make up a large part of His character? And since all of this is true, wouldn't you naturally expect that He will continue to treat you in the same manner in the days ahead?

In the prayer above, David is making an appeal to the Lord based on His past record. It is as if he has approached the bar in a judicial setting and brought forward some precedent the Court had established through past judicial decisions. "Lord, You have clearly established your methods of dealing with me. I plead the Court's mercy on the grounds of past precedent."

The next time you are in need of God's help in some situation, you might consider employing the same sanctioned tactics David used in prayer.

And how about you?

- *Has your past interactions with the Lord established a fixed trust in your heart for Him?*
- *When you have needed God's help, have you ever thought to remind Him of His past dealings with you?*

Kingdom Structure

*"I warned the proud to cease their arrogance! I told
the wicked to lower their insolent gaze... For promotion
and power come from nowhere on earth, but only from
God. He promotes one and deposes another."*
(Psalm 75:4, 6-7 LB)

"Power corrupts, and absolute power corrupts absolutely," goes the old maxim. Even the most superficial study of the Egyptian pharaohs, Roman emperors, British kings or even Catholic popes shows the truth of this statement. It is simply in the heart of man to be ambitious, and once his ambitions have been rewarded with a position of authority, for that position to corrupt him.

This is even true—albeit to a much lesser extent—within the evangelical Church hierarchy. Unquestionably, there are many fine men and women in positions of Christian leadership. But by and large the evangelical system is built upon ambition and talent. Those in the forefront are often those who want to be in that position and have the charisma and abilities to take them there. While such people tend to float to the top, there are many very humble and godly ministers who are relegated to less prominent positions.

While Christians are part of this tangible Church structure, there is another structure that is hidden to our eyes. It is God's kingdom on earth. In that organization, authority is meted out perfectly to those who truly deserve it. "[God's] throne is founded on two strong pillars—the one is Justice and the other Righteousness. Mercy and Truth walk before you as your attendants." (Psalm 89:14 LB) Yes, every aspect of a person's character—down to the *nth* degree—is taken into account by God. He sees it all plainly and clearly. With great precision He understands a person's spiritual makeup.

There are many men and women of God who will never receive accolades during their stay on earth, but they are clearly recognized for what they are in that unseen realm. In that parallel world, they are loved and respected in heaven, and feared in hell.

It is true that the Lord allows unworthy men to take for themselves positions of outward honor in the Church. But it will not be that way in heaven. Every believer will be seen for exactly who he truly is. In that fair land, there will be no human ambition, no devilish pride and no unjust appointments. It will be ruled perfectly by a God whose very throne is supported by Justice and Righteousness.

AND HOW ABOUT YOU?

- *What is the reality of your life in God? Do you attempt to present yourself as being further along than you actually are?*
- *Do you ever strive for the "chief seat?" Or are you content to be recognized by God alone?*

Week Ten: THURSDAY

Blessings and Prosperity

> *"There are many who pray: 'Give us more blessings, O Lord. Look on us with kindness!' But the joy that you have given me is more than they will ever have with all their grain and wine." (Psalm 4:6-7 GNB)*

The flesh of man insists upon believing a lie and devils do everything within their power to advance that lie. The world has built its entire reward system upon that lie. What is this lie? The false premise at the root of all of this is that carnal pleasures satisfy. The apostle John summed up all of these earthly allurements under three basic categories: the lust of the flesh, the lust of the eyes and the pride of life.

As I write this devotional I am 57-years-old and have been faithfully serving the Lord for some 25 years. If you were to ask me about the pleasures the world offers, I would immediately, sincerely and even fervently assure you that they simply do not have the intrinsic ability to satisfy a person. I know this in my mind; I even know this in my heart, and yet, there is another voice within me that insists that they can and will satisfy.

There are entire movements within the evangelical community that insist this falsehood is true. Their sermons are built upon the supposition of our verse: "Give us more blessings, O Lord. Look on us with kindness!" In Proverbs, Agur said it this way: "The leech has two daughters, 'Give,' 'Give.'" He went on to add: "There are three things that will not be satisfied, four that will not say, 'Enough': Sheol, and the barren womb, earth that is never satisfied with water, and fire that never says, 'Enough.'" (Proverbs 30:15-16) I will add a fifth: people who think that pleasurable experiences, numerous possessions or a position of prominence will satisfy them. It is all a great lie.

David penned Psalm 4 at a time of great spiritual clarity and could see the reality of life properly. He knew full well that only the things of God can really bring inward fulfillment. And yet, even David, when he grew older, richer and more spiritually lax, forgot this basic spiritual truth. How else could one explain his actions with Bathsheba?

The *truth* is that you could have a new pleasurable experience everyday; you could go out and purchase some new toy every week; you could gain one promotion after another year after year, but none of it will bring you inner fulfillment. In fact, the *truth* is that the more you give yourself over to the pursuit of these unsatisfying trinkets, the more depleted and miserable you will become inside.

At this time in his life, David understood something that many believers never come to understand: all of the outward blessings and prosperity one could hope for in this world will not make a person happy. Just as true is the converse of this statement: a person could have none of the outward blessings of earth life and be full of joy within. I will conclude with a simple question that we should all be mindful of: Wouldn't it be wiser to pursue the spiritual life that produces inward fulfillment than the lust-driven lifestyle that seeks that ever elusive satisfaction this world offers?

- *Are you still stuck in the merry-go-round of seeking satisfaction from a world that simply cannot provide it?*
- *Or can you honestly say with David, "But as for me, my contentment is not in wealth but in seeing you and knowing all is well between us. And when I awake in heaven, I will be fully satisfied, for I will see you face to face." (Psalm 17:15 LB)*

Week Ten: FRIDAY

Sinners and Hypocrites

*"I will approve of those who are faithful to God
and will let them live in my palace. Those who are
completely honest will be allowed to serve me. No
liar will live in my palace; no hypocrite will
remain in my presence." (Psalm 101:6-7 GNB)*

For a period of time when David was a young man he was
employed by aides to King Saul to play his harp and sing
for him. In his favored position he was privy to the inner workings
of the monarch's court. He saw unscrupulous men like Doeg the
Edomite continually vying for the king's favor. They were ruthless
and would stop at nothing to satisfy their ambitions. Indeed, it was
corrupt men like these who poisoned Saul's mind with slanderous
thoughts toward David. Yet, while it lasted, David's time in the king's
court served as valuable training for when he himself would sit on
the king's throne.

Eventually, in God's timing, David was installed as the monarch
of Israel. After forty years of languishing under the tyrannical reign of
Saul, the Jewish people were ready for a fresh start.

Excitement filled the air when the new "administration" was
established. David had a God-given vision for how to set up this
theocratic government. He created a "presidential cabinet" with
entire divisions under their care. New positions were now open in
the areas of military, administration, domestic service and even as

religious workers. Opportunities ranged from top and mid-level management all the way down to simple workers.

The words quoted above that David penned may have even been his way to serve notice across the land as to the type of people he wanted in his employ. He wanted to fill his government with sincere people who truly loved the Lord.

Nevertheless, David knew from experience that ambitious men would clamor for his favor. "I do not have fellowship with tricky, two-faced men; they are false and hypocritical," he wrote at another time. "I hate the sinners' hangouts and refuse to enter them." (Psalm 26:5-6 LB)

These were the two groups of people he wanted to avoid at all cost: religious pretenders and flagrant sinners.

Undoubtedly, shameless sinners would know better than to attempt to win his favor. Even if a brazen reprobate were to attempt to gain access to the king, his sharp eye would instantly spot him.

No, the ones David feared were those who were adept at hiding their true intentions behind a warm smile and flattering lips. Some hypocrites are so skilled in their ways that even the most discerning eye cannot easily detect them. Such people have a strong instinct as to what others want to hear from them. They are spiritual chameleons who instinctively know how to color their appearance to fit into any group. These charlatans are the ones with which David had the most concern. Everything a hypocrite says is carefully weighed to reinforce the image he wishes to convey to those around him.

You and I are not being swamped with people who want to ingratiate themselves with us, but, nevertheless, we should share David's heart when he wrote, "I want the company of the godly men and women in the land; they are the true nobility." (Psalm 16:3 LB)

AND HOW ABOUT YOU?

- *What kind of people fill your inner circle of friends?*

- *Are they known for having a heart after God, or do they seem to be pretenders and hypocrites? We all tend to become like those we fellowship with. If your closest friends are insincere, they will drag you down spiritually.*

- *Have you ever had to forfeit a friendship because you saw that it was dragging youdown spiritually?*

Remember

*"I recall the many miracles he did for me so long ago. Those
wonderful deeds are constantly in my thoughts. I cannot
stop thinking about them. O God, your ways are holy.
Where is there any other as mighty as you? You are the
God of miracles and wonders! You still demonstrate
your awesome power." (Psalm 77:11-14 LB)*

Aspah touched upon one of the most important features of a godly
life: engaging in a regular habit of recounting the many kind
acts God has done for him.

Let me briefly approach this great truth from a negative standpoint
first. To forget what God has done for you not only fosters a spirit of
ingratitude, but it also diminishes a person's faith. What is faith if it isn't
the awareness of God's involvement in our daily lives? Those who do
not take the time or make the effort to consider what the Lord has done
for them in the past will usually not have the faith to believe what He can
do for them today or in the future.

This was one of the monumental mistakes the children of Israel made
in the wilderness. They constantly lived in the circumstances of the *Now*.
When things looked difficult, rather than recounting the awesome things
the Lord had done to rescue them from Egypt and provide for them in
the wilderness, they would panic and complain. In fact, in the very next
psalm Asaph pointed out that the Hebrews "forgot His deeds and His
miracles that He had shown them." (Psalm 78:11)

But let's consider this passage from a positive perspective. When you take the time to really meditate upon the things God has done for you in the past, you are opening the eyes of your heart to His involvement in your life. This is one of the most powerful tools a believer has at his disposal to expand his faith. Furthermore, thanking the Lord for all of these many acts of kindness is one of the key ways you have to express your love to Him. What better way to express one's love to the Lord than recognizing His goodness and thanking Him for all He has done?

On a more practical note, I would suggest that you mentally (or on paper) categorize what God has done for you. Perhaps it would do you well to sit down right now and spend at least ten minutes thinking about your life before you came to Christ. Do you remember the sense of being lost? Do you remember the misery and hopelessness that was your daily lot? Have you ever really thought through all that the Holy Spirit must have done to steer you toward the things of God? And then there is all He has done since you became a believer! Surely these are all subjects worthy of consideration.

AND HOW ABOUT YOU?

- *Do you regularly recount the mighty things the Lord has done in your life?*
- *Do you ever spend time thanking Him for the way He has cared for your soul?*
- *Have you ever considered how important hindsight is in truly recognizing and appreciating God's workings in your life?*

Perspective of God

*"I will praise the name of God with song and magnify
Him with thanksgiving." (Psalm 69:30)*

If you were to express in a sentence or two what you believe about God, what do you think you would say? Is it possible your statements would reflect the typical canned sentiments that are passed around the Church without a great deal of thought? Allow me to rephrase the question. If God were to strip away all of the religious jargon that clutters our thinking on such issues and were to look deep in your heart, what would He discover about your opinion of Him? I offer this as a theoretical question, but it is actually what the Lord sees when He looks at you and me every minute of every day.

Most of us would make some grand statement such as: "God is full of love and possesses omnipotent power." Do you really believe that? *Really?* The fact is that the reality of what we think of God is shown in the way we live our lives. If we think He is full of love for us and has all the needed power to care for us, then we would live in great faith.

The truth is that, deep down in the recesses of our hearts, most of us have very low perspectives of God. A friend of mine sums up the attitude many have by saying, "God is like me, just a little bigger." Since our comprehension of His love is rather superficial, we can easily think of it on our own, human terms: "Like me; just a little bigger, or just a little better."

People don't tend to magnify the Lord, they tend to minimize Him. To magnify something means either to use a lens that makes something bigger than it really is (such as a microscope would do) or to see something far away in its actual size (which is what binoculars do). When it comes to seeing God, what we need are spiritual binoculars.

A minister once said that many people look through the wrong end of the binoculars of life. Those things that should be seen as big are minimized while unimportant things are made to seem huge.

When God is given His rightful position in a person's heart, the person tends to see life in its proper proportions. So when the psalmist exhorts us to magnify the Lord, he is telling us that if we will do this, we will give the important matters of life their proper due and we will not allow petty things to distort our vision.

How exactly do we magnify the Lord? God is so overwhelming in every one of His attributes that all we have to do is to think about Him. For instance, consider His infinitude. The next time you have a clear sky and a dark night, spend some time looking up into the heavenlies and meditate upon the great Being who holds it all in the palm of His hand. Just doing little exercises like this will magnify the Lord in your mind's eye.

AND HOW ABOUT YOU?

- *Do you ever take the time and make the effort to meditate upon the character and attributes of God?*
- *Perhaps you would consider making a list of His attributes and committing yourself to spend some time during the next week contemplating them one by one.*

Notes

WEEK

ELEVEN

Thoughts Too High for a Fool

> *"How magnificent is thy creation, Lord, how unfathomable are thy purposes! And still, too dull to learn, too slow to grasp his lesson, the wrong-doer goes on in his busy wickedness." (Psalm 92:5-6 Knox)*

The psalmist here touches on the two primary aspects of God's mighty works: His creation of the enormous realm of Nature and His providential dealings with mankind.

"Magnificent" is an apt term to employ when considering the Lord's efforts in Creation. It doesn't require a lot of mental exertion to see what a massive undertaking this was. For instance, consider how the animal and aquatic kingdoms, the insect world and the realm of vegetation all work together in beautiful harmony. Each and every individual species of plants and animals have been perfectly created to function on earth's environment. An analysis of any single form of creation is an astounding study on how the Lord fashioned it to procreate and survive on our planet.

And yet it is amazing that the scientific community is blind to what the Creator has accomplished! For instance, I stand amazed when I consider how the Lord provided camels with feet that expand out to great webs capable of walking on the scorching, shifting sands of the desert; and when I think about how our God gave these same camels the capacity to drink and store enormous amounts of water to sustain them in the barren wastelands, I can only look on with admiration and wonder! "What diversity, Lord, in thy creatures! What wisdom has designed them all! There is nothing on earth but gives proof of thy creative power." (Psalm 104:24 Knox)

The typical scientist—who in his arrogance refuses to acknowledge God—ponders the same animal and can only say that it has gone through a series of mutations over millions of years until it developed its own particular abilities to survive. These men never seem to have an answer as to how the species survived before it acquired these necessary abilities! And they have absolutely no scientific facts to substantiate their claims! They begin with the supposition that there is no God, and since there is no God, this must be how all of this came into being.

The same holds true of the history of mankind. God has been unfolding His marvelous purposes in man for some six thousand years. The realm of Time serves as a backdrop for the Lord to play out all of His great plans for human beings. Earth life has been created to serve a probationary function so that individuals can decide for themselves whether or not they will submit themselves to the Lordship of Christ. Each person who has ever lived—the small and great, the gifted and ungifted, the rich and the poor—every man, woman and child has the opportunity to enjoy all of the temporal and eternal benefits of living for God.

But because the human species has been so thoroughly corrupted by sin, he does not have the capacity within himself to do the right thing. But this too was figured into God's great plan. What did He do? He arranged for His own Son to come to this planet to provide His life as an atonement for man's sin and failure. God's solution was to implant His own Spirit within man's heart to live the life of godliness

He demanded of His people. This too is a thought too high for fools who have blinded themselves to the truth. They don't want to believe any of this because they are unwilling to humble themselves before God in contrition and repentance.

AND HOW ABOUT YOU?

- *Are you too busy with earth life to consider the "magnificent" works and "unfathomable" purposes of God?*

- *Take some time today and pick out some aspect of Nature and meditate on how God fit it into His glorious plan for earth.*

- *You might also spend time considering how the Lord has worked out His glorious plans for mankind.*

Week Eleven: TUESDAY

Revive Me

"I lie defeated in the dust; revive me, as you have promised."
(Psalm 119:25 GNB)

L arry is tired. Day after day he drags himself through life. He has no energy and no motivation for the things of God. He is suffering from a paralyzing lethargy. He begins asking God to energize him. "Please Lord, this infernal listlessness is robbing me of life!"

He doesn't realize it, but his cries to God are falling on deaf ears. Why? Because he has the answer right in his own hands: "His divine power has granted to us everything pertaining to life and godliness…" (2 Peter 1:3) Is it the Lord's fault if Larry fails to appropriate God's provision for his dilemma?

Let me say illustrate it this way. The human body has been created with basic rules of operation. Experience is our owner's manual. We know full well that if we eat too much sugar or too many simple carbohydrates, our energy is going to be depleted. We fully understand that if we stay up late at night, so that we don't get the sleep we need, we will have to drag ourselves through the activities of the following day. We can cry out to God all day long, but if we abuse our bodies like this He is not going to magically energize us. The solution to that problem is a nutritional diet and healthy sleep habits.

The same basic principle holds true for spiritual lethargy. If we are languishing in the spiritual doldrums, it is almost certainly because we are not taking proper care of our souls. Allow me to ask some pointed questions:

- Are you nourishing your soul with the Word of God, or are you depleting it with too much worldly entertainment?

- Are you becoming stimulated toward the things of God through a daily prayer time, or are you attempting to survive in the godless culture around you by your own efforts?

- Are you living in obedience to the Lord at the heart level, or are you content to obey a few outward "rules" of Christianity?

I think you get the point. The Lord has given you all the tools you need to live a healthy spiritual life. There is no reason you should be spiritually apathetic. Don't be like "Lazy Larry"; rouse yourself into action right away! Implement the weapons the Lord has equipped you with in your battle with the world, the flesh and the devil. You have everything you need to live a joyful and fruitful life if you will only live by the rules of spiritual health.

And how about you?

- *Have you been guilty of complaining to the Lord that He hasn't done enough to "revive" you when you haven't fulfilled your own obligations? Praying for revival is a good thing so long as you are doing your part to live a healthy Christian life.*

Week Eleven: WEDNESDAY

Sanctioned Trouble

> *"In my prosperity I said, 'This is forever; nothing can stop me now! The Lord has shown me his favor. He has made me steady as a mountain.' Then, Lord, you turned your face away from me and cut off your river of blessings. Suddenly my courage was gone; I was terrified and panic-stricken." (Psalm 30:6-7 LB)*

In this psalm, David perfectly articulates the great challenge the Lord faces in His dealings with the fickle nature of man. Even the godliest saints are prone to such wild vacillations of temper!

The title of Psalm 30 tells us that it was a song written "at the dedication of the house of David." It seems that the psalmist king penned it upon the completion of his own palace in Jerusalem. Those were heady days for the young monarch. David was beginning to enjoy the unmixed blessings of God upon his life:

Then... they built a house for David. And David realized that the Lord had established him as king over Israel... Meanwhile David took more concubines and wives from Jerusalem, after he came from Hebron; and more sons and daughters were born to David." (2 Samuel 5:11-13)

As much as the Lord thoroughly enjoys blessing His people, He knows far better than we do that our tendency is to turn away from Him when prosperity flourishes. The Lord is a master at mixing blessings with griefs, mountain-top experiences with the mundane nature of the daily life. He knows just when to shut one off and turn on the other.

Times of blessing are an integral part of the Christian life. We all need the encouragement of feeling God's presence, of receiving tokens of His kindness, of being able to enjoy some of the positive aspects of life on earth. No one can endure nonstop hardship. We all need those times of blessing to encourage us along the way.

Yet, even more important from an eternal standpoint is our great need to suffer adversity and hardship. It is through the difficulties of life that we become humbled and sanctified. Hard times are what shape us into Christ's image. Affliction also deepens our perspective of the spiritual realm. We are all terribly shallow by nature; only grief can bring about the maturity to be able to comprehend the more profound things of life.

David was doing well—everything was going his way—and yet trouble was on the way: "When the Philistines heard that they had anointed David king over Israel, all the Philistines went up to seek out David…" (2 Samuel 5:17)

Not only did he face a brutal horde of murderous pagans intent upon his destruction, but then the sense of God's presence suddenly seemed to vanish! "Then David inquired of the Lord…" (2 Samuel 5:17) This was what God had in mind all along. David was probably becoming a little too self-confident. In one day, he was thrown into the kind of panic that sent him running to his God.

And how about you?

- *Do you tend to live in self-reliance?*
- *Can you see how the Lord has had to alternate blessings and discipline in your life?*
- *Have you ever made an earnest effort to recount His dealings in your life and thank Him for them?*

A World Without God

> *"There is no God above us, is the fond thought*
> *of reckless hearts..."* (Psalm 53:1 Knox)

In that classic movie, "It's a Wonderful Life," an angel shows George Bailey what life would be like in his hometown of Bedford Falls had he never been born. Without George's influence, there was nothing to hinder the greedy ambitions of old man Potter. He was able to buy up one business after another until he owned virtually the entire town. In fact, he became so powerful that he renamed it "Pottersville." Instead of the quiet, family-friendly village he had grown up in, George was shown a decadent township boasting bars and strip-clubs. Even decent folks he had known had been thoroughly corrupted by the environment. Such was the effect on this community of one honest man.

In their arrogance and rebellion, atheists believe that there is no God; that the world was formed by some kind of cosmic explosion billions of years ago. They want to believe this because they do not want to be held accountable for their actions.

Little do such fools know what that would actually mean. What would this world be like if there wasn't a God of love tempering Satan's activities?

God oversees everything that occurs on our planet, of course, but there have been certain locales and periods of history where the enemy has had greater sway. If you would like to know what this world would be like without the Lord's influence, consider some of the following examples.

ENTERING HIS COURTS

During the War years, the Nazi regime brought out the very worst in people who lived in Germany and the other nations it conquered. Jews had lived peacefully for many years in the "Fatherland" before Hitler came to power. Under the Führer's leadership, German culture became infused with a national mindset of Jew hating. The Nazi party could not have accomplished the destruction of six million Jews without the voluntary aid of thousands of civilians.

Another example: the small African nation of Uganda underwent a similar transformation under the leadership of Idi Amin. With his Nubian supporters, the savage dictator brutally murdered 300,000 people.

Some fifteen years after the overthrow of his government, the Hutu tribe in neighboring Rwanda instituted a systematic genocide of their rivals, the Tutsis. By the end of 1994, some 800,000 people—whose only crime was that of belonging to a different tribe—lay slaughtered in the villages of Rwanda.

These are but a handful of examples of what happens when people groups allow Satan to fill their culture with his malice and hatred. What would it be like on Earth if God was completely absent? Only a visit to hell could answer such a question.

AND HOW ABOUT YOU?

- *Do you ever doubt the existence of God? The next time you allow your mind to wander into such forbidden territory, just consider what this world would be like if He weren't keeping the devil's malice in check.*
- *Do you believe your life is a check against evil in your community, even if you can't cite specific examples?*

Praise the Lord!

> *"Praise the Lord! Oh give thanks to the Lord,*
> *for He is good; for His lovingkindness*
> *is everlasting." (Psalm 106:1)*

"**P**raise the Lord" is one of those catch-phrases that is used regularly in Christian circles. Sometimes I wonder if the original meaning of it has been lost along the way, though.

The meaning of the word "praise" (Heb. *halal*) is connected to the idea of something shining, and it came to be used about people who would brag about their own positive attributes. For instance, in another psalm David wrote that "the wicked boasts (*halal*) of his heart's desire." (Psalm 10:3) And Solomon said, "Let another praise (*halal*) you, and not your own mouth; a stranger, and not your own lips." (Proverbs 27:2)

So when the psalmist tells us to "praise the Lord," he isn't saying that we should simply repeat a phrase we have heard; he is letting us know that we should speak openly and often to others about God's wonderful qualities.

In yet another psalm David wrote, "My soul shall make its boast in the Lord; the humble shall hear it and rejoice." (Psalm 34:2) Had he really said all that he meant, perhaps he would have said something along these lines: "If I had a mind to, I could boast about the time that I killed that nine foot giant; I could tell you about the victories I have won for God's kingdom; I could point out all the many rich psalms

I have written. But do you know what? The only boasting I want to do is about what a great God I serve! He made all of this happen!"

A thousand years later the apostle Paul summed up his feelings on the subject when he told the Galatians: "But may it never be that I would boast, except in the cross of our Lord Jesus Christ, through which the world has been crucified to me, and I to the world." (Galatians 6:14) Having been afforded the greater revelations of seeing what God Incarnate did at Calvary, Paul understood even better than David that man has nothing in himself worth bragging about; the only good that we can lay claim to is what Jesus Christ accomplished on our behalf at Calvary.

AND HOW ABOUT YOU?

- *Can you say that you too have had the revelation that our only claim to anything good in ourselves is what Christ has done for us?*

- *Does that revelation provoke despair or worship in your heart? Some who have a hard time accepting the fact that there is no good in them may drift into despair, but if we see our condition in the Light of Christ, the result should be heart-felt praise!*

Notes

~Notes~

A Harvest of Light

"A harvest of light is sown for the righteous,
and joy for all good men." (Psalm 97:11 NEB)

L ight is one of the great metaphors presented in Scripture. While darkness represents Satan and all of the confusion, distress and evil of his kingdom, light is a fit emblem of the Lord and the great family of God.

The apostle John said that "God is Light, and in Him there is no darkness at all. " (1 John 1:5) James simply called Him "the Father of lights" (James 1:17), while the apostle Paul said He "dwells in unapproachable light." (1 Timothy 6:16) The Psalmist said that He covers Himself with light as with a cloak. (Psalm 104:2) So whatever else may be said about light, we know that, at the very least, God is the source of it. Light emanates from His being, from His throne and from His kingdom.

One of the unmistakable attributes of light is that it shows believers how to proceed on the journey of life. The psalmist wrote, "Thy word is a lamp to my feet, and a light to my path." (Psalm 119:105) He also said, "The unfolding of Thy words gives light; it gives understanding to the simple." (Psalm 119:130) Solomon wrote that "the path of the righteous is like the light of dawn, that shines brighter and brighter until the full day." (Proverbs 4:18)

The fact is that we are on a lifelong journey through a dark and treacherous world. We desperately need God's light to show us the way, to reveal truth and expose falsehood, to illuminate the entirety of our inner being: heart, mind and soul.

One of the great principles of the Kingdom is that a man shall reap what he sows. It is a clear-cut truth that definite consequences—whether good or bad—will accompany our actions. Our subject verse above presents a similar principle, albeit with one noteworthy difference: the godly do not sow the "harvest of light" themselves but it is sown on their behalf. It is as if a band of angels goes along with them on their path, scattering seeds of spiritual light in front of them, around them and in their wake. Not only are they blessed with light for their own lives, but they become the means for light to be spread upon other lives as well. Those seeds of light—like sparks flying off a grinder—will be scattered all about them. Such seeds will eventually bring forth a harvest.

AND HOW ABOUT YOU?

- *What is the depth and breadth of light in your life?*
- *Are you content with a shallow degree of light, or do you feel yourself being compelled to bathe yourself in it?*
- *I can assure you of this: the greater the light has shone in your heart, the greater the harvest that will come forth from your life.*

Week Eleven: SUNDAY

The Cost of Idolatry

*"Troubles multiply for those who chase after other gods. I
will not take part in their sacrifices of blood or even speak
the names of their gods." (Psalm 16:4 NLT)*

I suppose if you traveled into some of the tribal regions of Africa
or India you could find people who still bow down to physical
idols, but this is a form of devil worship which is now generally confined
to primitive cultures.

Even in New Testament times, the meaning of idolatry was
already in transition. The Romans and Greeks had their mythological
gods who were represented by statues, but the apostles were already
looking past the physical, literal concept of idols to the propensity
within the human heart to prostrate itself before "images of desire."
For instance, Paul said that covetousness was tantamount to idolatry.
(Ephesians 5:5; Colossians 3:5)

Whatever the case may be, it is commonly held among Bible scholars
that the concept of idolatry extends beyond the ancient practice of
worshiping a carved pole or a little statue to allowing anything to take
God's rightful place in a person's heart.

I once preached a message entitled, "America: Land of Idols."
I wish I could say that those who were guilty of idolatry in that
congregation really responded with heartfelt repentance. But
unfortunately, it was one of those churches where most of the
people refused to hear the truth being presented. Perhaps when I had

concluded that message, the Holy Spirit said, "Leave them alone, they are joined to their idols." (Hosea 4:17) If we could see what is going on in the unseen realm around us, I suspect the consequences of being given over to the pursuit of some idol would appear terrifying to us.

The truth is that America is a land of idols. Our prosperity and technological advances have provided an enormous variety of ways a person can indulge his flesh. There is no end to the idols people have to choose from.

Consider Psalm 16:4 from the following translations:

- Those choosing other gods shall be filled with sorrow. (LB)
- Those who rush to other gods bring many troubles on themselves. (GNB)
- What do they do but lay up fresh store of sorrows, that betake themselves to alien gods? (Knox)

The wording is different but the meaning is the same: pursuing interests that displace one's passion for God brings a world of grief. John said it simply and said it best: "Little children, guard yourselves from idols." (1 John 5:21) May it never be said of any of us: "Leave him alone, he is joined to his idols."

And how about you?

- *What idols have you overcome in your life?*
- *Do you still find yourself longing to give place to those worldly allurements? Or have you allowed the Lord to thoroughly eradicate them from your heart?*

Notes

WEEK
TWELVE

Howling Dogs

"Back come they at nightfall, like yelping dogs,
and prowl about the city; far and wide they will roam in
search of their prey, and snarl with rage when they
go unfed at last." (Psalm 59:15 Knox)

One of the most eerie things a person can hear when alone in the woods at night is a pack of howling, screaming coyotes. There have been a number of times over the years that I have heard one of these packs yelping nearby when on one of my early morning prayer walks in the woods. In Kentucky, these roaming canine gangs are actually a mixture of coyotes and wild dogs. They overwhelm their victims with a relentless, swarming assault. The very confusion they bring makes their lethal attacks all the more effective.

Such dog packs serve as an apt metaphor for the demonic realm. The activity of unclean spirits can be summed up in three basic categories: allurements, accusations and assaults. Whichever approach they choose, their attacks can be overwhelming and unnerving.

Satan is called "the tempter." (Matthew 4:3) Enemy agents work in close connection with our flesh to lure us into sin. (Matthew 26:41; James 1:14) Temptations abound in the world around us; every one of them attempting to entice us off the Narrow Path and away from God. The enemy can defeat believers with devastating sins like illicit sexual activity or a number of less consequential sins like unmerciful attitudes. They know their victims' propensities well and fashion their enticements accordingly.

Once a person has caved in to some temptation (whether it involves a major transgression or a minor sin), the enemy is right there to accuse the person of being a false Christian. Satan is called the "accuser of the brethren" for a reason. (Revelation 12:10) Demons point the finger of condemnation at struggling believers to discourage them in the midst of battle. They know all too well that if they can bury a Christian in despair, they can get him to give up. "What's the use!" some faltering believers lament. "I can't live up to these high standards. I might as well throw in the towel!"

The final method these demonic hordes use to defeat believers is to attack them through other people. Throughout the history of the Church there have been periods when the devil has managed to get someone who is fully under his sway into a position of absolute power. Whenever this occurs, the persecution of God's people is sure to follow. However, this sort of thing happens on a smaller scale in the lives of Christian individuals all the time. Some believers dread going to their jobs because of taunting coworkers or bosses who are hostile to them because of their faith.

AND HOW ABOUT YOU?

- *What kind of plots does the enemy hatch against your faith?*
- *How does he tempt you?*
- *How does he accuse you?*
- *How does he attack you? Ask God to grant you the protection you need against all of his assaults.*

Week Twelve: TUESDAY

Unchanging Realities

"They are corrupt, they have committed abominable deeds;
there is no one who does good." (Psalm 14:1b)
"Forever, O Lord, Your word is settled
in heaven." (Psalm 119:89)

For the first 5,800 years of mankind's existence, people lived extremely simple lifestyles. This began to change in the Industrial Age which was ushered in during the 1800's. But who could have imagined the dramatic changes to people's lives that would occur during the 20th Century? The tranquil pace of life that was in place in the beginning of that monumental century would give way to a frantic way of life by the end of it. This all occurred because of the enormous strides mankind made in the realm of knowledge.

Yet, with all of the improvements technology and science have brought to our lives, nothing has diminished the moral and spiritual realities taught in Scripture. I will touch on but a couple of them.

The first thing that has not changed is the nature of man. The Age of Enlightenment has not weakened man's propensity toward sin. In fact, the great technological advancements made during the past hundred years have made it easier for people to indulge the sins of their flesh. For instance, consider young people who lived on farms at the turn of the 20th Century. Yes, of course, they could find ways to become involved in sinful activities, but the truth is that not many did. By the end of the century, radio, television and the internet made all kinds of sinful activity easily available to them. For all of science's strides forward, they have not come up with a solution to man's tendency to transgress God's laws.

There is another thing that has not changed: the Word of God. In spite of the many attacks it has suffered from mockers, skeptics and God-haters, the Bible remains the one constant source of Truth on this dark planet. The truths taught in Scripture are every bit as relevant today as they were when they were written. Man has not changed; nor have his spiritual needs changed. The Bible contains every answer that people need no matter how modern their problems may be. The reason this is true is that the underlying issue with drug, pornography and gambling addictions, or any other ungodly behavior, is sin, and the Bible is the only source of Truth that has the wherewithal to address it.

For all of the physical improvements we have enjoyed during our lifetimes, we still must deal with our spiritual needs. Thank God that His Word remains relevant and powerful for the greatest needs we will ever face.

AND HOW ABOUT YOU?

- *Have you considered the enormity of man's greatest need?*
- *Have you reflected upon the fact that the Bible still has the answers for mankind's problems even though it was written so long ago?*

~Notes~

~Notes~

The Problem with Whitewashing

"There was a time when I wouldn't admit what a sinner I was. But my dishonesty made me miserable and filled my days with frustration." (Psalm 32:3 LB)

Let's face it: nobody likes to admit being wrong. The difference between true believers and pseudo-Christians very much hinges on whether or not they are willing to acknowledge and turn from their sins. Oh, people are willing to acknowledge sin in a general way, but invariably do their utmost to avoid humbly admitting to specific acts of sin. Only the Lord can tell the difference between true and false conversions (and that really isn't what I want to touch on here).

Instead, I want to talk about the way believers conduct themselves in daily life. I believe this is an important spiritual principle: the level of a person's life in God is directly tied to the degree he or she has allowed the Lord to deal with their sinful nature. The only way a person can be full of God is to first be emptied of Self. This primarily happens through the process of repentance.

Jesus told the Pharisees that they were like "whitewashed tombs." He went on to say, "So you, too, outwardly appear righteous to men, but inwardly you are full of hypocrisy and lawlessness." (Matthew 23:27-28) In other words, rather than allowing the Lord to really deal with their sinful natures, they "whitewashed" their lives with a superficial façade of godliness.

They were full of the spirit of hypocrisy—the mentality that they could act as though they were really walking with God while keeping the Holy Spirit at arm's length. "...holding to a form of godliness, although they have denied its power..." the apostle Paul would later say. (2 Timothy 3:5) They were content to be spiritual fakes.

For all of their minute rules and regulations, the Pharisees were actually full of lawlessness. They did not want God telling them what to do. They were willing to maintain the image of righteousness but were unwilling to fight for the real thing.

There was a period of David's life when he lapsed into this kind of falsehood, but when the misery of his hypocrisy became too much to bear, he collapsed in a heap of godly sorrow over his sin. Thank God we can always repent!

AND HOW ABOUT YOU?

- *Have you been allowing the Lord to deal with your sinful tendencies, selfish attitudes and wrong motives?*
- *Or have you been content with putting on an act of godliness while keeping the door of your heart closed to the Lord?*

Low and Vulgar Things

"I will try to walk a blameless path, but how I need your
help, especially in my own home, where I long to act as
I should. Help me to refuse the low and vulgar things..."
(Psalm 101:2-3 LB)

One day loved ones will gather around our graves to pay their final respects. The presiding minister will either have the happy privilege of being able to point to our lives as clear-cut examples of what the Christian life should be, or he will have the unhappy task of exaggerating our good qualities and graciously sidestepping the truth about what we were really like.

Family members know the real story, of course. They are generally the ones who know the reality of a person's profession of faith. The psalmist here seems to understand that our spirituality is first marked by our lifestyle at home.

I believe one of the real benchmarks of the lives of Christians today is how they handle all of the many temptations that come with television and the internet. The standard of righteousness within the Christian population of the United States has dropped so low that hardly anyone believes that they need to guard themselves from the kind of gross sin depicted in normal television programming. So long as they aren't seeing actual nudity they are quite content to view all kinds of carnality and worldliness.

I suspect if this psalmist was transported into our time and could sit down with a typical Christian family as they gather around the TV set, he would be stunned at what they were shamelessly viewing. Consider this phrase in some other translations; allow the redundancy of these words to penetrate your heart:

- I refuse to take a second look at corrupting people and degrading things… (MSG)
- I will set no base thing before mine eyes… (DeW)
- I will not have anything unworthy in my presence… (Har)
- I will not allow a base thought to attract my attention… (Ber)

This man obviously lived a very righteous life with God. He refused to allow the ungodly culture in which he lived to shape and influence his life. He did his utmost to shun and avoid every form of sin.

And how about you?

- *If this man dropped in for a visit to your home, what would he find?*
- *Would he see sincere believers who are walking "a blameless path?*
- *Or would he discover those who regularly compromise with what they know to be sinful and worldly?*

The Shortness of Life

> *"O Lord, help me understand my mortality and the*
> *brevity of life! Let me realize how quickly my life will pass!*
> *Look, you make my days short-lived, and my life span is*
> *nothing from your perspective. Surely all people, even those*
> *who seem secure, are nothing but vapor." (Psalm 39:4-5 NET)*

Considering how much can be crowded into a single day—appointments, phone calls, errands, meals, sleep and so on—and then multiplying all of that by the tens of thousands of days we have been allotted, it could make a person wonder what David must have been thinking when he talked about his entire life span being "nothing."

He certainly must not have written this when he was a young man and his life seemed to extend on endlessly in his future. Very few young people ever consider the prospect of death because it seems to be such a remote experience. He must not have written this when he was in the prime of his life, when he was conquering kingdoms and building a nation. Who could have time to think about death when in the midst of all of that activity?

No, he must have written this toward the end of his life when his days seemed to rush by, hastening him on to his deathbed. At that point in life, the years of a person's life can seem like a mere passing vapor. Where did all of that time go?

It seems that David's prayer is that he might live his daily life with a greater awareness of the value of time. We have all been allotted a certain amount of this precious commodity and we should treat it as a gift from God.

"What will I accomplish with the time afforded to me that will hold any meaning in eternity?" David seems to be asking himself. He wanted to live his life with the sobriety that question provokes.

Perhaps a good gauge of my life can be seen by the way I lived my life yesterday. That 24-hour period gave me opportunities to live for self or live for God; to live frivolously or to live soberly; to redeem my time or to squander it. What will that day look like from the perspective of eternity?

Chances are it was a fairly accurate picture of my lifetime. For what is one's life but an accumulation of yesterdays? Not many people consider such deep subjects but I believe it is a worthwhile question to ponder.

And how about you?

- *Do you ever consider the way you are spending your time?*
- *Would you say that you are making good use of your time for the Lord?*
- *Or do you think you are squandering a good deal of it in meaningless activity?*

Week Twelve: SATURDAY

Wisdom's Starting Point

*"For as high as the heavens are above the earth, so great
is His lovingkindness toward those who fear Him. As far
as the east is from the west, so far has He removed our
transgressions from us. Just as a father has compassion
on his children, so the Lord has compassion on
those who fear Him." (Psalm 103:11-13)*

Psalm 103 is one of those pinnacles of encouragement found
deposited throughout Scripture. It is a virtual treasure house
of promised blessings. If God's people had no other promises to hold
onto in life, there would be enough here to keep them going for the rest
of their lives.

Yet, as is true in nearly all biblical promises, they are attached to
conditions. Interestingly, when presumptuous people read such passages,
all they can see are the promises. Their eyes seem to be blinded to the
stipulations which accompany them. They read the words, but they
don't sink in. They latch onto the positive statements to the disregard
of everything else.

In the case of the three verses quoted above, David enumerated
three great assurances to God's people: abundant lovingkindness to be
showered upon their lives, total forgiveness of sin and a father's compassion
on their struggles. What Bible-believing person wouldn't be buoyed by
such promises? And those who fulfill the attached condition should be
encouraged by this pledge from God.

Perhaps David sensed the tendency of some people to overlook the fact that these promises are only extended to those who fear the Lord because he repeats this stipulation a few verses later.

I think David understood better than most that the fear of the Lord is a vital component in a believer's life. Until it has become established within a person's heart, he will never really grasp the need to obey God. He might fulfill some rules that are observable to those around him, but his obedience will always be shallow and meaningless.

A.W. Tozer once said, "The truth is that salvation apart from obedience is unknown in the sacred Scriptures… Apart from obedience, there can be no salvation, for salvation without obedience is a self-contradictory impossibility. The essence of sin is rebellion against divine authority."

And, in light of the passage of Scripture we are examining, I would add that apart from the fear of the Lord there will be no true obedience. Perhaps that is why another psalmist would later exclaim, "The fear of the Lord is the beginning of wisdom…" (Psalm 111:10)

And how about you?

- *Can you see how living with a deep concern about pleasing God is a vital part of one's relationship with Him?*
- *Would you say that your life reflects someone with a fear of the Lord? If so, appropriate these promises as your own for you are the very person they were extended to!*

Hallelujah!

"Hallelujah! Praise God in his holy sanctuary; give praise in the mighty dome of heaven." (Psalm 150:1 NAB)

"Praise him for his mighty achievements, praise him for his transcendent greatness." (Psalm 150:2 JB)

"Praise Him with trumpet sound; praise Him with harp and lyre." (Psalm 150:3 NASB)

"Praise him with drums and dancing. Praise him with harps and flutes." (Psalm 150:4 GNB)

"Praise him with the clang of the cymbals, the cymbals that ring merrily." (Psalm 150:5 Knox)

"Let everything that has breath praise the Lord. Praise the Lord!" (Psalm 150:6 NASB)

I will conclude this devotional with the insightful words of the following writers:

"This noble close of the Psalter rings out one clear note of praise, as the end of all the many moods and experiences recorded in its wonderful sighs and songs. Tears, groans, wailings for sin, meditations on the dark depths of Providence, fainting faith and foiled aspirations, all lead up to this. The psalm is more than an artistic close of the Psalter: it is a prophecy of the last result of the devout life, and, in its unclouded sunny-ness, as well as in its universality, it proclaims the certain end of the weary years for the individual and for the world."—Alexander MacLaren[1]

"All living things in the air, the earth, the waters. Let there be one universal burst of praise... Thus, at the end of all the trials, the conflicts, the persecutions, the sorrows, the joys recorded in this book, the psalmist gives utterance to feelings of joy, triumph, transport, rejoicing; and thus at the end of all - when the affairs of this world shall be closed - when the church shall have passed through all its trials, shall have borne all its persecutions, shall have suffered all that it is appointed to suffer - when the work of redemption shall be complete, and all the ransomed of the Lord shall have been recovered from sin, and shall be saved - that church, all heaven, the whole universe, shall break forth in one loud, long, triumphant Hallelujah."—Albert Barnes[2]

"Join all ye living things in the eternal song. Be ye least or greatest, withhold not your praises. What a day will it be when all things in all places unite to glorify the one only living and true God! This will be the final triumph of the church of God. *'Praise ye the Lord.'* Once more, Hallelujah! Thus is... the Book of Psalms ended by a glowing word of adoration. Reader, wilt not thou at this moment pause a while and worship the Lord thy God? Hallelujah!"—Charles Spurgeon[3]

Notes

ENDNOTES

WEEK ONE

1. Samuel Chadwick, as quoted by Revival Library, accessed at *http:// www.revival-library.org/leadership/rq_prayer.php* on August 30, 2012.

2. Watchman Nee, *Let Us Pray,* (New York, NY: Christian Fellowship Publishers 1977) p. 20.

3. Charles Spurgeon, *The Treasury of David,* Psalm 57:8, e-Sword, www.e-sword.net.

WEEK THREE

1. Charles Spurgeon, *The Treasury of David*, Psalm 34:21, e-Sword, www.e-sword.net.

2. H.D.M. Spence, *The Pulpit Commentary, Vol. 1,* (Grand Rapids, MI: Wm. B. Eerdmans Publishing Company, 1950) p. 80.

3. *ibid.*

WEEK FOUR

1. Alexander MacLaren, as quoted by Marcus Dod, *An Exposition of the Bible: A Series of Expositions Covering the Books of the Old and New Testament, Volume 3,* (Hartford, CT: S.S. Scranton Co., 1907) p. 139.

2. Charles Spurgeon, *The Treasury of David,* Psalm 51:6, e-Sword, www.e-sword.net.

3. Thomas Horton, *The Biblical Illustrator,* Psalm 51:17, as cited in AGES Digital Library (Rio, WI: AGES Software Inc., 2001).

4. J. J. Stewart Perowne, *The Biblical Illustrator,* Psalm 51:17, as cited in AGES Digital Library (Rio, WI: AGES Software Inc., 2001).

Entering His Courts

Week Five

1. Albert Barnes, *Albert Barnes' Notes on the Bible,* Psalm 39:6, e-Sword, www.e-sword.net.

Week Six

1. Adam Clarke, *Adam Clarke's Commentary on the Bible,* Psalm 2:3, e-Sword, www.e-sword.net.

2. Albert Barnes, *Albert Barnes' Notes on the Bible,* 1 Peter 1:12, e-Sword, www.e-sword.net.

Week Seven

1. Charles Spurgeon, *The Treasury of David,* Psalm 1:5, e-Sword, www.e-sword.net.

Week Nine

1. Charles Spurgeon, *The Treasury of David,* Psalm 50:16-17, e-Sword, www.e-sword.net.

Week Twelve

1. Alexander MacLaren, as quoted by Marcus Dod, *An Exposition of the Bible: A Series of Expositions Covering the Books of the Old and New Testament, Volume 3, (*Hartford, CT: S.S. Scranton Co., 1907) p. 139.

2. Albert Barnes, *Albert Barnes' Notes on the Bible,* Psalm 150, e-Sword, www.e-sword.net.

3. Charles Spurgeon, *The Treasury of David,* Psalm 150, e-Sword, www.e-sword.net.

The Walk Series...

THE WALK OF REPENTANCE

EXPERIENCE THE TIMES OF REFRESHING THAT FOLLOW REPENTANCE

The one thing believers in America don't need more of is information about Christianity. We know more about it than any people who have ever lived. Our problem isn't a lack of knowledge. Our problem is a lack of living it.

This 24-week Bible study has impacted the lives of thousands of people because it equips them to live out the Word of God. It is a simple, straightforward discipleship tool that focuses on the basics of the Christian life. Each week of this easy-to-use curriculum has a theme, addressing the challenges of the Christian life one step at a time.

Whether used by individuals, small groups or couples, in counseling settings, Sunday school classes or prison ministry, *The Walk of Repentance* makes a profound impact and leads sensitive hearts into a deeper intimacy with the Lord.

$15.99

Volume discounts available. Call 888-PURELIFE for specific pricing.

WHETHER USED INDIVIDUALLY OR COLLECTIVELY,
EACH OF THESE BIBLE STUDIES IS A GREAT TOOL FOR
PERSONAL GROWTH OR GROUP DISCIPLESHIP.

A LAMP UNTO MY FEET

A 12-week journey through the beautiful
Psalm 119 and the life of David.
You will be brought into a deeper love,
respect and appreciation for God's Word.
$10.99

PRESSING ON TOWARD THE HEAVENLY CALLING

The apostle Paul's Prison Epistles are
a divine archive of profound revelations about
the kingdom of God. This 12-week Bible study
will challenge you to reach for the abundant life
in God that Paul testifies is available
to every one of us.
$10.99

HE LEADS ME BESIDE STILL WATERS

A practical study of the choicest Psalms.
This 12-week Bible study takes you right into
the intimate interactions between pious men and
a loving, caring God and evokes a determined
desire to find His Presence for yourself.
$10.99

SAVE when you buy all three! Only $25.99
www.purelifeministries.org

Pure Life Ministries

Pure Life Ministries helps Christian men and women achieve lasting freedom from sexual sin. The Apostle Paul said, "Walk in the Spirit and you will not fulfill the lust of the flesh." Since 1986, Pure Life Ministries (PLM) has been discipling Christians into the holiness and purity of heart that comes from a Spirit-controlled life. At the root, illicit sexual behavior is sin and must be treated with spiritual remedies. Our counseling programs and teaching resources are rooted in the biblical principles that, when applied to the believer's daily life, will lead him out of bondage and into freedom in Christ.

Biblical Teaching Resources

Pure Life Ministries offers a full line of books, audio CDs and DVDs specifically designed to give Christians the tools they need to live in sexual purity.

Residential Care

The most intense and involved counseling PLM offers comes through the **Live-In Program** (6-12 months), in Dry Ridge, Kentucky. The godly and sober atmosphere on our 45-acre campus provokes the hunger for God and deep repentance that destroys the hold of sin in men's lives.

Help At Home

The **Overcomers At-Home Program** (OCAH) is available for those who cannot come to Kentucky for the Live-In program. This twelve-week counseling program, which is also available for struggling women, features weekly counseling sessions and many of the same teachings offered in the Live-In Program.

Care For Wives

Pure Life Ministries also offers help to wives of men in sexual sin. Our wives' counselors have suffered through the trials and storms of such a discovery and can offer a devastated wife a sympathetic ear and the biblical solutions that worked in their lives.

Pure Life Ministries
14 School St. • Dry Ridge • KY • 41035
Office: 859.824.4444 • Orders: 888.293.8714
info@purelifeministries.org
www.purelifeministries.org